KS2 Success

Age 9-10

Maths

Paul Broadbent

10-Minute Tests

Sample page

clear instructional text

topic being covered

test number for quick reference

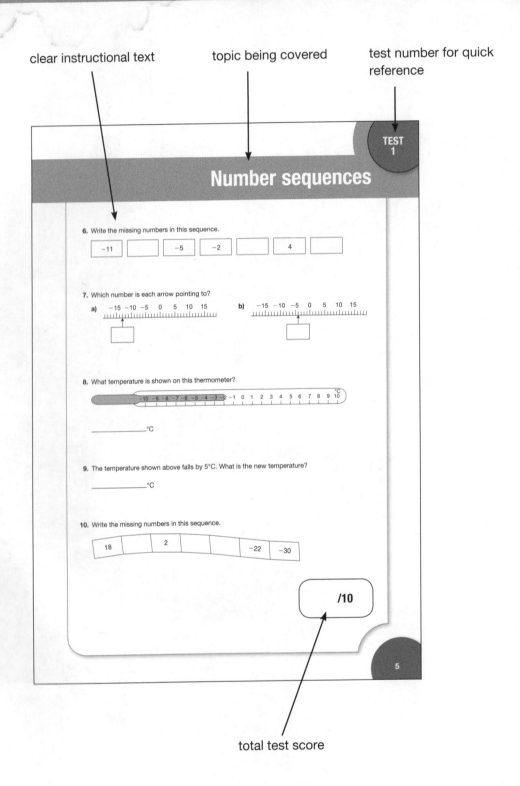

TEST 1

Number sequences

6. Write the missing numbers in this sequence.

| −11 | | −5 | −2 | | 4 | |

7. Which number is each arrow pointing to?

a) −15 −10 −5 0 5 10 15

b) −15 −10 −5 0 5 10 15

8. What temperature is shown on this thermometer?

°C
−10 −9 −8 −7 −6 −5 −4 −3 −2 −1 0 1 2 3 4 5 6 7 8 9 10

_____ °C

9. The temperature shown above falls by 5°C. What is the new temperature?

_____ °C

10. Write the missing numbers in this sequence.

| 18 | | 2 | | | −22 | −30 |

/10

5

total test score

Contents

Number sequences

1. Write the next three numbers in this sequence.

| 63 | 74 | 85 | 96 | | | |

2. Write the missing numbers in this sequence.

| 14 | | 2 | −4 | −10 | | |

3. Which number is each arrow pointing to?

a)

−15 −10 −5   0   5   10   15

b)

−15 −10 −5   0   5   10   15

4. What temperature is shown on this thermometer?

°C
−10 −9 −8 −7 −6 −5 −4 −3 −2 −1 0 1 2 3 4 5 6 7 8 9 10

_____°C

5. The temperature shown above rises by 6°C. What is the new temperature?

_____°C

Number sequences

6. Write the missing numbers in this sequence.

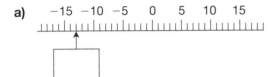

| −11 | | −5 | −2 | | 4 | |

7. Which number is each arrow pointing to?

a) −15 −10 −5 0 5 10 15

b) −15 −10 −5 0 5 10 15

8. What temperature is shown on this thermometer?

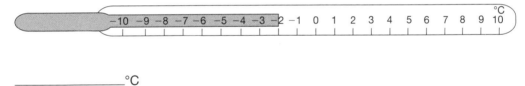

−10 −9 −8 −7 −6 −5 −4 −3 −2 −1 0 1 2 3 4 5 6 7 8 9 10 °C

_____°C

9. The temperature shown above falls by 5°C. What is the new temperature?

_____°C

10. Write the missing numbers in this sequence.

| 18 | | 2 | | | −22 | −30 |

/10

Decimals

1. Draw lines to match the decimals to the fractions.

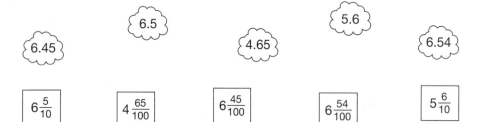

2. Write the decimals indicated by the arrows on this number line.

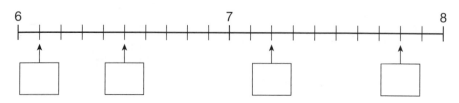

3. Write these fractions as decimals.

a) $\dfrac{34}{100}$ →

b) $\dfrac{19}{100}$ →

c) $\dfrac{7}{100}$ →

4. Change these decimals to hundredths.

a) 0.51 →

b) 0.92 →

c) 0.08 →

5. Rearrange each of these to make a decimal number as close to 4 as possible.

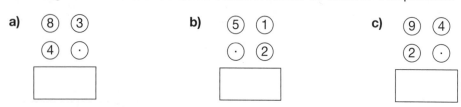

Decimals

6. Write the missing decimals indicated by arrows on this number line.

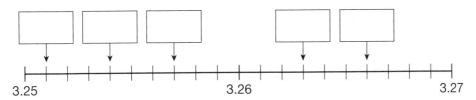

3.25   3.26   3.27

7. Write the value of the circled digits as tenths or hundredths.

    a)   8.⑨25 ➔_____

    b)   13. 11⑧ ➔_____

    c)   10. 0⑤5 ➔_____

8. Write these as decimals.

    a) $\frac{1}{1000}$ ➔ _____

    b) $\frac{21}{1000}$ ➔ _____

    c) $\frac{900}{1000}$ ➔ _____

9. Write this as a decimal number.

    $400 + 80 + 6 + \frac{7}{10} + \frac{9}{100} + \frac{5}{1000} =$ _____

10. Change these decimals to whole numbers and thousandths.

    a)   6.249 ➔ _____

    b)   3.021 ➔ _____

    c)   7.555 ➔ _____

/10

Ordering numbers

1. Write the sign < or > for each pair of numbers.

   a) 20056 _____ 20506

   b) 39989 _____ 39898

2. Circle the largest number in each pair.

   a) 745.5   745.09

   b) 36.85   36.58

   c) 1207.14   1270.03

3. Write these numbers in order, starting with the smallest.

   (29945)   (208865)   (29906)   (208956)   (290030)

_____

4. Tick the smallest amount in this set.

   35.78 kg ☐   30.19 kg ☐   35.8 kg ☐   30.3 kg ☐   30.47 kg ☐

5. Write <, > or = between each pair of decimals.

   a) 0.011 _____ 0.111   b) 0.42 _____ 0.402   c) 0.658 _____ 0.568

Ordering numbers

6. These temperatures should be in order, starting with the lowest temperature.
   Colour the two temperatures that have been swapped.

 −10°C −1°C −4°C −7°C 2°C 5°C

7. Write these lengths in order, starting with the shortest.

   (37.45 m)   (38.33 m)   (37.91 m)   (38.3 m)   (37.5 m)

   _____

8. These are the costs of five train tickets. Write the prices in order, starting with the most expensive.

   £38.70

   £31.29

   £74.88   £40.05

   £60.90

   _____

9. Write the number that is halfway between each pair.

   a)   5000   10 000   b)   0   50 000

   [ ]   [ ]

10. Write these temperatures in order, starting with the lowest.

    −17°C   3°C   0°C   −19°C   −11°C   −20°C

    _____

    /10

Rounding and approximating

1. Draw lines to join these numbers to the nearest 10.

| 6535 | | 6575 | | 6548 | | 6556 | | 6573 |

6530   6540   6550   6560   6570   6580

2. Round these numbers to the nearest 1000.

    a) 16 869 → _____   b) 28 055 → _____   c) 49 344 → _____

3. Round these numbers to the nearest pound.

    a) £18.48 → _____   b) £27.52 → _____   c) £49.61 → _____

4. Write two decimal numbers that would round to 12 as the nearest whole number.

[   ] and [   ]

5. Round each of these to the nearest 100 g.

a) 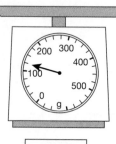 [   ] g

b) 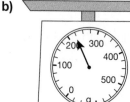 [   ] g

c) 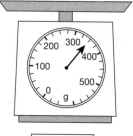 [   ] g

Rounding and approximating

6. Estimate how much liquid is in this jug in millilitres.

_____ ml

7. Circle the number that is nearest to the correct answer for each of these.

a)   144 + 262 =   350   400   450

b)   352 − 147 =   200   250   300

8. Round each number in these calculations to the nearest 10 to give an approximate answer.

a)   1438 + 327   →   _____

b)   1902 − 578   →   _____

9. Draw lines to join these decimals to the nearest whole number.

| 52.83 | | 52.08 | | 55.19 | | 53.51 |

10. Approximately how many hours are there in February in a leap year? Circle the correct range.

100–200 hours   300–400 hours   600–700 hours   800–900 hours

/10

Fractions, decimals and percentages

1. Write these as improper fractions.

a)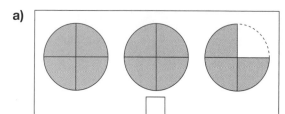

$\dfrac{\square}{4}$

b)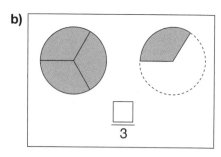

$\dfrac{\square}{3}$

2. Change these improper fractions to whole numbers and fractions.

a) $\dfrac{9}{2}$ = _____

b) $\dfrac{15}{4}$ = _____

c) $\dfrac{18}{5}$ = _____

d) $\dfrac{20}{3}$ = _____

3. Complete this table to show the matching fractions, decimals and percentages.

Fractions	Decimals	Percentages
$\dfrac{1}{2}$		50%
	0.2	
		75%
$\dfrac{3}{10}$		

4. Write the percentage of the grid that is shaded.

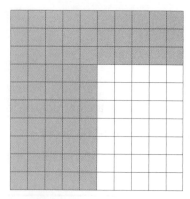

_____%

5. Write these fractions as percentages.

a) $\dfrac{35}{100}$ = _____

b) $\dfrac{1}{4}$ = _____

c) $\dfrac{40}{50}$ = _____

Fractions, decimals and percentages

6. Colour these scales to show each percentage.

a)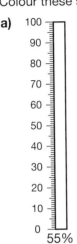
55%

b)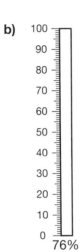
76%

7. Draw lines to join the matching fractions, decimals and percentages.

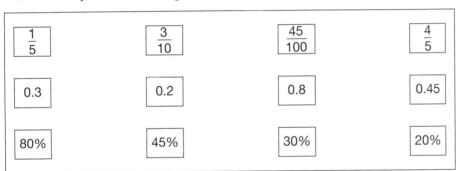

| $\frac{1}{5}$ | $\frac{3}{10}$ | $\frac{45}{100}$ | $\frac{4}{5}$ |

| 0.3 | 0.2 | 0.8 | 0.45 |

| 80% | 45% | 30% | 20% |

8. Write these percentages as fractions.

a) 90% = ☐/☐

b) 5% = ☐/☐

c) 60% = ☐/☐

9. Use > or < to complete these.

a) 0.8 _____ 8%

b) 0.2 _____ 50%

c) 0.25 _____ 75%

10. Change these to improper fractions.

a) $4\frac{3}{4}$ → ☐/☐

b) $2\frac{1}{2}$ → ☐/☐

c) $5\frac{2}{3}$ → ☐/☐

/10

Equivalent fractions

1. Write each fraction indicated by the matching shaded areas, in two ways.

a)

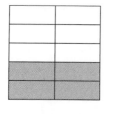

$$\frac{\Box}{\Box} = \frac{\Box}{\Box}$$

b)

 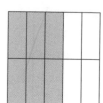

$$\frac{\Box}{\Box} = \frac{\Box}{\Box}$$

2. Cross out the fraction that is not equivalent.

a)

$$\frac{3}{4} \rightarrow \quad \begin{array}{cc} \dfrac{12}{16} & \dfrac{6}{8} \\[2mm] \dfrac{15}{20} & \dfrac{14}{16} \end{array}$$

b)

$$\frac{2}{3} \rightarrow \quad \begin{array}{cc} \dfrac{4}{6} & \dfrac{6}{9} \\[2mm] \dfrac{12}{25} & \dfrac{8}{12} \end{array}$$

3. Complete this equivalent fraction chain.

$$\frac{2}{5} = \frac{4}{\Box} = \frac{\Box}{15} = \frac{8}{\Box} = \frac{\Box}{25}$$

4. Write the fraction shaded, using the smallest possible denominator.

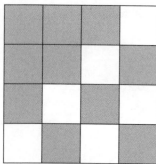

_____

5. Complete these equivalent fractions.

a)

$$\frac{3}{10} = \frac{\Box}{50}$$

b)

$$\frac{5}{6} = \frac{15}{\Box}$$

c)

$$\frac{2}{3} = \frac{40}{\Box}$$

Equivalent fractions

6. Shade $\frac{2}{3}$ of this circle.

7. Write down the fraction shaded on this shape. Then work out the equivalent fraction with the smallest possible denominator.

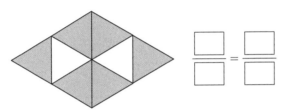

8. Complete this equivalent fraction chain.

$$\frac{5}{8} = \frac{\boxed{}}{16} = \frac{15}{\boxed{}} = \frac{\boxed{}}{32} = \frac{25}{\boxed{}}$$

9. Simplify each fraction so that you have the smallest possible denominator.

   a) $\frac{6}{15} = \frac{\boxed{}}{\boxed{}}$

   b) $\frac{25}{100} = \frac{\boxed{}}{\boxed{}}$

   c) $\frac{14}{16} = \frac{\boxed{}}{\boxed{}}$

10. Write four different fractions that are equivalent to $\frac{3}{5}$.

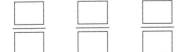

/10

Colour these tile patterns to match the ratios.

1. The ratio of red to blue is one to every three.

2. The ratio of green to yellow is one to every four.

3. The ratio of black to white is three to every five.

4. In a cake recipe, 25 g of cherries are needed for every 100 g of raisins. What weight of cherries is needed for a cake that has 800 g of raisins?

_____ g

5. What proportion of this grid is shaded? Give your answer as a fraction, using the smallest possible denominator.

Ratio and proportion

6. In a group of 20 children, 12 are girls and 8 are boys. What proportion of the group are girls? Write your answer as a fraction, using the smallest possible denominator.

7. This is a recipe for six people. Write out the ingredients needed for just two people.

Fish Pie (for six people)	Fish Pie (for two people)
600 g fish	_____ g fish
1.5 kg potatoes	_____ g potatoes
300 g peas	_____ g peas
240 g cheese	_____ g cheese
120 g butter	_____ g butter
180 ml milk	_____ ml milk

8. What is the ratio of grey to white tiles? Give the ratio in its simplest form.

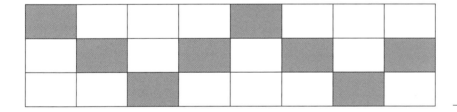

_____

9. In a book of 40 pages, two out of every five of the pages have a picture on them. How many pages have a picture?

_____

10. 12 red beads and 16 white beads are kept in a bag. What is the ratio of red to white beads? Give the ratio in its simplest form.

_____

/10

Multiplication and division facts

1. Write the missing numbers.

   a) 7 × _____ = 56

   b) _____ × 9 = 54

   c) 4 × _____ = 32

2. Complete these multiplication grids.

   a)

×	7	9	6
8			
7			
4			

   b)

×	10	11	12
8			
9			
10			

3. Answer these.

   a) 27 ÷ 3 = _____

   b) 42 ÷ 6 = _____

   c) 56 ÷ 7 = _____

4. Which two numbers less than 50 can be divided exactly by 2, 3, 4, 6, 8 and 12?

   _____   _____

5. Draw lines to join each division to its matching remainder.

   | 25 ÷ 3 | | 44 ÷ 5 | | 68 ÷ 9 | | 51 ÷ 8 | | 44 ÷ 6 |

 1   2    3   4   5

Multiplication and division facts

6. Write two different multiplications for each answer. Do not use the number 1 and, in each answer, you must use four different numbers.

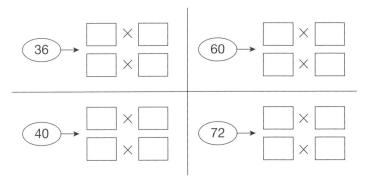

7. Complete these multiplication grids.

a)

×	9		6
3			
8		40	
			42

b)

×	7	4	
8			64
		36	
			24

8. Write the missing numbers.

a)   30 × _____ = 180

b)   _____ × 4 = 200

c)   50 × _____ = 350

9. I am thinking of a number. If I divide it by 6 and then add 2, the answer is 7. What number am I thinking of?

_____

10. I am thinking of a number. If I multiply it by 8 and then subtract 2, the answer is 30. What number am I thinking of?

_____

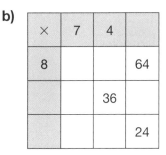

/10

Factors and multiples

1. Write the factors of these numbers in order.

    a) 32 → | 1, 2, |

    b) 20 → | |

    c) 25 → | |

    d) 55 → | |

2. Answer these.

    a) The 5th multiple of 4 is… _____.

    b) The 6th multiple of 3 is… _____.

    c) The 4th multiple of 9 is… _____.

3. Write the three smallest numbers that will fit into the central shaded part of each Venn diagram.

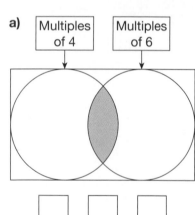

    a) Multiples of 4   Multiples of 6

    b) Multiples of 3   Multiples of 5

4. Write the factors of these numbers in pairs.

    a) 28 → (1, 28) _____

    b) 45 → _____

    c) 40 → _____

    d) 24 → _____

5. 3 is a factor of 123. Tick the correct answer.

    True ☐   False ☐

Factors and multiples

Use this set of numbers to answer questions 6–8.

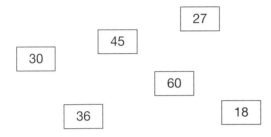

27

45

30

60

36   18

6. Which three numbers are multiples of both 3 and 5?

_____   _____   _____

7. Which two numbers are multiples of 9, but not multiples of 6?

_____   _____

8. Which number is a multiple of 2, 3, 4, 5, 6 and 10?

_____

9. Circle the correct answer.

a)

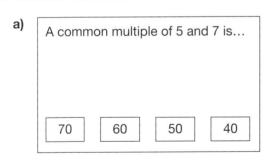

A common multiple of 5 and 7 is...

| 70 | 60 | 50 | 40 |

b)

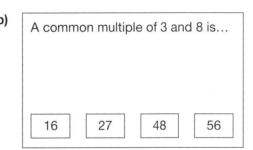

A common multiple of 3 and 8 is...

| 16 | 27 | 48 | 56 |

10. 17 is a prime number. Tick the correct answer.

True ☐   False ☐

How do you know?

/10

Addition

1. Answer these.

   a) 108 + 53 = _____

   b) 125 + 91 = _____

   c) 146 + 72 = _____

2. Four pairs of these numbers each total 5000. Write the pairs.

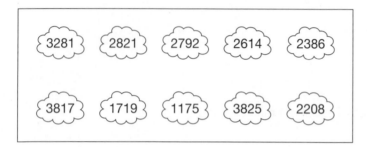

   _____ and _____   _____ and _____

   _____ and _____   _____ and _____

3. Answer these.

   a)   4 1 4 7   b)   3 2 0 9   c)   5 2 3 8   d)   6 3 6 4
        + 2 1 6 4   + 1 1 5 8   + 4 1 8 5   + 5 2 7 7
        _____   _____   _____   _____

        _____   _____   _____   _____

4. What is the perimeter of this shape?

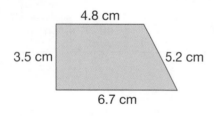

   4.8 cm
   3.5 cm
   5.2 cm
   6.7 cm

   _____ cm

Addition

5. Add each row and column to find the total in the bottom right-hand corner.

7.2	9.1	
6.4	8.9	

6. Answer these.

a)   1 4 1 0 5
        + 3 2 6 3 9
        _____

b)   2 7 6 8 2
        + 4 1 5 0 8
        _____

c)   5 3 8 5 7
        + 2 4 7 9 4
        _____

7. Sam goes shopping and spends £37.45 on a pair of trainers and £18.99 on a tracksuit. How much does he spend in total?

£ _____

8. Write the missing digits.

a)   ☐ 3 1 5
      + 1 5 ☐ 2
      _____
         9 8 7 7

b)   4 8 2 9
      + 3 ☐ 5 ☐
      _____
         7 9 8 1

c)   4 ☐ 2 9
      + 2 7 ☐ 3
      _____
         7 0 2 2

9. Draw lines to join pairs of numbers that total £30.

£18.75   £11.25   £10.25   £15.85

£12.55   £19.75   £14.15   £17.45

10. Write the missing digits.

3 ☐ 9 + 7 ☐ ☐ = 4 2 5

/10

Subtraction

1. Draw lines to join pairs with a difference of 88.

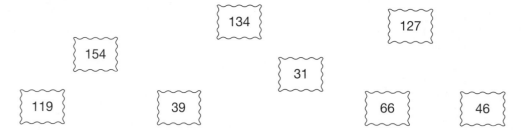

134   127

154

31

119   39   66   46

2. Answer these.

a)
```
  3 0 2 9
− 1 3 6 2
─────────
```

b)
```
  5 6 1 4
− 2 7 9 5
─────────
```

c)
```
  7 2 0 4
− 4 9 1 6
─────────
```

3. Write the change from £10 for each of these.

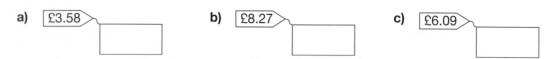

a) £3.58

b) £8.27

c) £6.09

4. Write the missing digits.

a)
```
  3 8   1
− 1 ☐ 9
─────────
  2 3 ☐
```

b)
```
  4 ☐ 8
− ☐ 9 3
─────────
  1 8 5
```

c)
```
  6 0   4
− 3 ☐ 5
─────────
  ☐ 2 ☐
```

5. I am thinking of a number. If I subtract 255 from it, the answer is 89.
What number am I thinking of?

_____

Subtraction

This diagram shows the distances by road of some cities from London in kilometres.

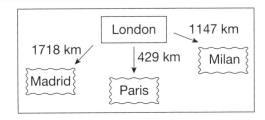

6. How much further is it from London to Madrid than from London to Paris?

_____ km

7. How much further is it from London to Madrid than from London to Milan?

_____ km

8. Answer these.

a)   6 3 2 1 5
     − 2 0 9 4 3
     _____

b)   4 0 3 8 7
     − 1 9 4 7 9
     _____

c)   8 3 0 1 6
     − 5 6 1 7 8
     _____

9. Write the difference between each pair.

a)

_____ litres

b)

_____ litres

10. A plank of wood is 2.14 metres in length. It is cut into two pieces. If one of the pieces is 0.79 metres, what is the length of the other piece?

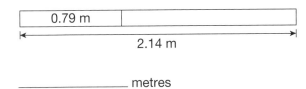

_____ metres

/10

Multiplication

1. Double each of these numbers.

a) 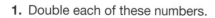 316 → ⬚   b) 185 → ⬚   c) 259 → ⬚

2. This is a ×80 machine. Complete the table.

IN	6		3		9
OUT		560		400	

3. Tick the multiplication that has the largest product.

78 × 4	57 × 6	94 × 3	48 × 7
☐	☐	☐	☐

4. Answer these. Show your method in the boxes below.

a)   159 × 6 = ⬚

b)   374 × 8 = ⬚

5. A magazine costs £3.48 per month. What is the cost for six months' subscription to the magazine?

£ _____

£3.48

Multiplication

6. Answer these. Show your method in the boxes below.

a) $38 \times 49 =$ ☐

b) $57 \times 26 =$ ☐

7. What is the area of each of these rectangles?

a)

17 cm

12 cm

Area = ☐ cm²

b)

23 cm

19 cm

Area = ☐ cm²

8. A box weighs 28 kg. What is the weight of 15 boxes?

_____ kg

9. Answer these.

a)
$$\begin{array}{r} 1\,3\,7\,4 \\ \times \qquad 8 \\ \hline \\ \hline \end{array}$$

b)
$$\begin{array}{r} 3\,2\,0\,9 \\ \times \qquad 6 \\ \hline \\ \hline \end{array}$$

c)
$$\begin{array}{r} 5\,4\,7\,8 \\ \times \qquad 4 \\ \hline \\ \hline \end{array}$$

10. What is the product of 425 and 19?

_____

/10

Division

1. Answer these. Show your method in the boxes below.

   a) 67 ÷ 4 = [   ]

   b) 106 ÷ 3 = [   ]

2. Write the missing numbers in each of these.

   a) _____ ÷ 8 = 15

   b) _____ ÷ 3 = 19

3. This is a ÷100 machine. Complete the table.

IN → ÷100 → OUT

IN	490		245		705
OUT		3.7		6.81	

4. Answer these.

   a) 6)384

   b) 5)295

   c) 7)791

5. Tick the numbers that are not exactly divisible by 3.

143	219	171	206	316	378
☐	☐	☐	☐	☐	☐

Division

6. A tube holds six tennis balls. How many tubes are needed for each of these quantities of tennis balls? Some of the tubes may not be full.

a) 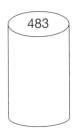 483

b)  566

c) 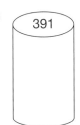 391

d) 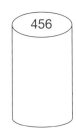 456

_____   _____   _____   _____

7. Answer these.

a) 4) 5 3 7 5   b) 5) 2 8 3 6   c) 3) 1 5 0 9

8. Write the missing digits to complete these.

a) 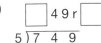 ☐ 4 9 r ☐
5) 7   4   9

b) 3 5 r ☐
8) ☐ 8 5
☐

c) 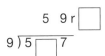 5   9 r ☐
9) 5 ☐ 7
☐

9. Which number between 90 and 100 has a remainder of 1 when it is divided by 8?

_____

10. What is the smallest number you can add to 490 to make it exactly divisible by 4?

_____

/10

Fractions and percentages

1. Answer each of these.

a)

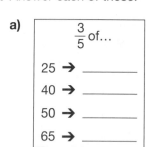

$\frac{3}{5}$ of...

25 → _____

40 → _____

50 → _____

65 → _____

b)

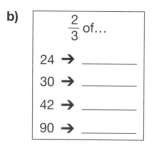

$\frac{2}{3}$ of...

24 → _____

30 → _____

42 → _____

90 → _____

2. Answer these.

a) 10% of £2 = _____

b) 25% of £20 = _____

c) 20% of £10 = _____

3. In a maths test, Emma scored 18 out of 20. The following week she scored 45 out of 50 in a different test. What were the percentage scores for each test?

a) $\frac{18}{20}$ = _____ %

b) $\frac{45}{50}$ = _____ %

4. What fraction of the grid is left white? Write it in its simplest form.

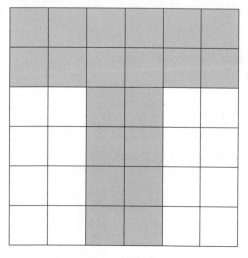

_____

5. What is $\frac{3}{4}$ of each of these?

a) 52 kg

b) 600 ml

c) 900 g

d) 120 cm

_____ kg

_____ ml

_____ g

_____ cm

Fractions and percentages

6. These are the ingredients for an 800 g cake. Write the weight of each ingredient.

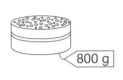

800 g

Recipe	
30% flour	
20% butter	
10% sugar	
25% raisins	
10% cherries	
5% walnuts	

Ingredients	
flour	_____ g
butter	_____ g
sugar	_____ g
raisins	_____ g
cherries	_____ g
walnuts	_____ g

7. Answer these.

a) 10% of £75 = ☐

b) 20% of £75 = ☐

c) 5% of £75 = ☐

d) 15% of £75 = ☐

8. A bag contains 60 marbles. $\frac{1}{3}$ of them are red, $\frac{2}{5}$ of them are blue and $\frac{1}{10}$ of them are yellow. The rest of the marbles are green. What fraction of the marbles in the bag are green?

_____

9. Circle the largest amount.

$\frac{5}{8}$ of 56 litres $\frac{4}{7}$ of 63 litres

10. What is 5% of each of these?

a) 80 kg → _____ kg

b) 30 kg → _____ kg

c) 140 kg → _____ kg

/10

Number puzzles

Write the missing numbers on each of these grids.

1.

5	+	3	=	
+		−		−
	+		=	
=		=		=
	−	3	=	5

2.

4	+	4	=	
+		×		−
	+		=	7
=		=		=
9	−		=	

3.

	+	6	=	
×		÷		−
3	×		=	
=		=		=
12	÷		=	4

4.

	÷		=	2
−		÷		×
	−	2	=	
=		=		=
4	×		=	12

5.

24	÷	6	=	
÷		×		×
	÷	2	=	
=		=		=
	×		=	24

6.

6	×		=	36
×		÷		÷
	×		=	6
=		=		=
	×		=	6

Arithmogons

In each of these, the number in the box is the total of the two numbers in the circles on either side. Write the missing numbers.

1. ③ —— ▢ —— ⑧

2.

⑤
▢   13
⑥ — ▢ — ○

3.

○ —— ▢ —— ⑧
16   ▢
⑨ —— 13 —— ○

4.

○ — 10 — ⑦
8   ▢   ▢
○ — 13 — ○

5.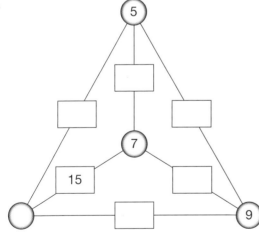

6.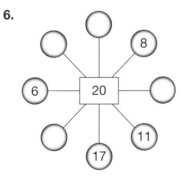

2-D shapes

1. Draw lines to match each name to the correct regular shape.

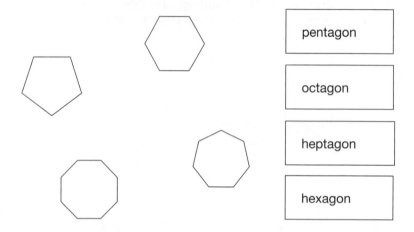

pentagon

octagon

heptagon

hexagon

2. Complete the table for these triangles.

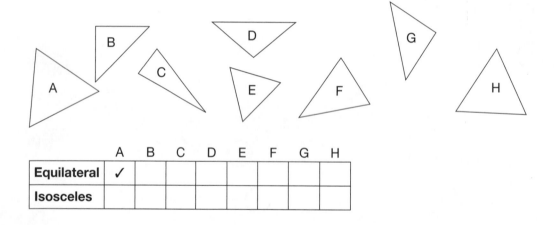

	A	B	C	D	E	F	G	H
Equilateral	✓							
Isosceles								

3. Which of the triangles above have a right angle? _____

4. An isosceles triangle has a line of symmetry. Is this always, sometimes or never true?

_____

5. What is the name of this shape?

   _____

2-D shapes

6. Draw lines to join each triangle to the correct place on the Venn diagram.

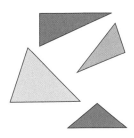
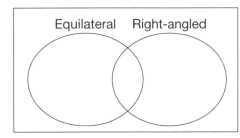
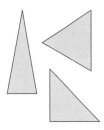

Equilateral   Right-angled

7. Draw a quadrilateral on this grid which has opposite sides of equal length but no right angles.

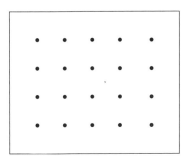

8. A quadrilateral is symmetrical. Is this always, sometimes or never true?

_____

9. Tick each shape that has parallel sides.

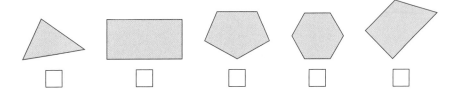

10. Draw a line perpendicular to AB from C.

A   C   B

/10

3-D shapes

1. Complete the table for these 3-D shapes.

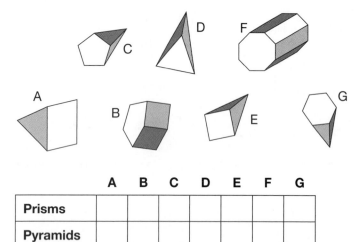

	A	B	C	D	E	F	G
Prisms							
Pyramids							

2. How many faces, edges and vertices does a cube have?

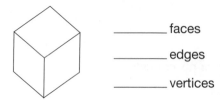

_____ faces

_____ edges

_____ vertices

3. Name the shapes made from each net.

a)

b)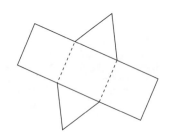

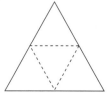

_____   _____

4. A pyramid has four faces. Is this always, sometimes or never true?

_____

5. How many vertices does a triangular prism have?

_____

3-D shapes

6. Tick the tetrahedron in this set of pyramids.

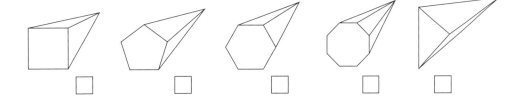

☐ ☐ ☐ ☐ ☐

7. How many edges does a tetrahedron have? _____

8. Name the shapes made from each net.

a)

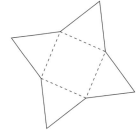

b)

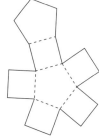

_____   _____

9. Name this 3-D shape.

_____

10. Draw a prism and a pyramid starting from a triangle.

a)

prism

b)

pyramid

/10

Position and direction

Write the position on the grid of each shape.

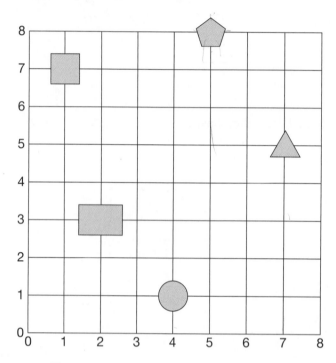

1. rectangle → (2, 3)

2. pentagon → (5, 8)

3. square → (1, 7)

4. triangle → (7, 5)

5. circle → (4, 1)

Position and direction

Each of these grids has a mirror line. Draw the reflection of each shape on the grid.

6.

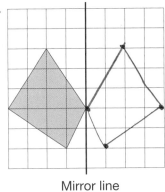

Mirror line

7.

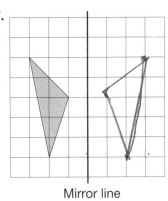

Mirror line

8.

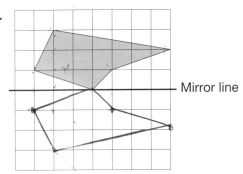

Mirror line

9.

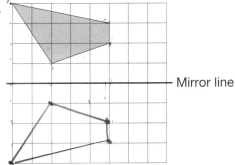

Mirror line

10. This grid has two mirror lines.

Draw the reflection of the shape.

Mirror line

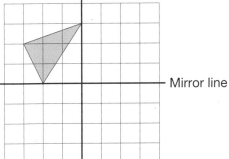

Mirror line

/10

Roman numerals

1. Write these as numbers:

   a) XI _____ b) XIX _____ c) XXI _____

2. Write these as Roman numerals:

   a) 17 _____ b) 24 _____ c) 29 _____

3. Write the missing Roman numerals on this clock:

4. Write < or > to make these true:

   a) XXXII _____ XXIV b) LXIII _____ LXX

5. XC is 90 in Roman numerals. Tick the correct answer.

   True ☐   False ☐

   Explain how you know.

Roman numerals

6. Write these in order, starting with the smallest:

LIV   LX   XLV   L   LVIII

_____

7. a) Write the missing numeral in this sequence:

DXXX   DXXXI   DXXXII   DXXXIII   _____   DXXXV   DXXXVI   DXXXVII

b) Write the missing Roman numeral as a number: _____

8.

The digits 6, 3 and 5 can make these numbers:

563 ⟶ DLXIII

653 ⟶ DCLIII

Make two more numbers from these three digits and write them as Roman numerals:

a) _____ ⟶ _____

b) _____ ⟶ _____

9. Circle the largest number:

DCCXVII   DCCXXIV

10. What year is shown by MMXV? _____

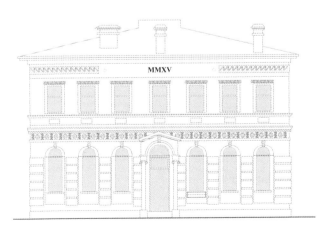

MMXV

/10

Angles

1. Tick all the acute angles in these shapes.

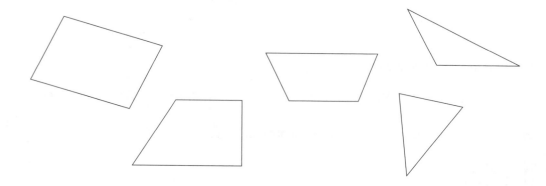

2. Draw an obtuse angle on this grid.

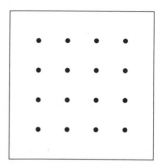

3. Estimate these angles. For each of the two angles, circle the angle in the box that is nearest your estimate.

a)

b)

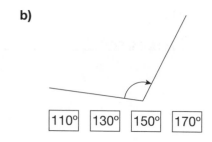

| 30° | 40° | 50° | 60° |

| 110° | 130° | 150° | 170° |

4. What is the interior angle sum of a rectangle?

_____

5. True or false? An obtuse angle is between 90° and 180°.

_____

Angles

6. Use a protractor or angle measurer to measure this angle.

7. What is the interior angle sum of an equilateral triangle? _____

8. How many degrees are there in three right angles? _____

9. Write the size of the missing angles on these straight lines. Do not measure the angles.

a)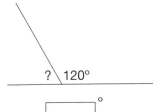

b)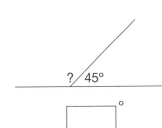

c)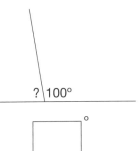

10. Write the size of the missing angles in these right angles. Do not measure the angles.

a)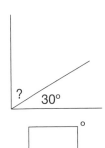

b)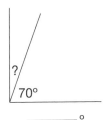

c)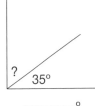

/10

Standard units of measure

1. Write these lengths.

a) 4.2 m   = _____ cm

b) 6.3 km = _____ m

c) 78 mm = _____ cm

d) 80 cm = _____ m

> Underline the amount each item is most likely to measure.

2. My bedroom is (3.8 cm) (3.8 m) (30.8 m) (3.8 km) across from one wall to the other.

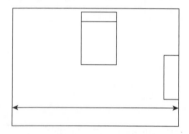

3. A loaf of bread weighs (85 g) (850 g) (8.5 kg) (8.5 g).

4. I put my (2.2 ml) (22 l) (22 ml) (2.2 l) carton of orange juice in the fridge.

5. Measure the length of this line in centimetres and in millimetres.

[   ] cm = [   ] mm

Standard units of measure

6. What is 850 m less than 6 km?

_____ km or _____ m

7. Complete these.

a) 6.7 kg = _____ g

b) 3.95 kg = _____ g

c) 8200 g = _____ kg

d) 4750 g = _____ kg

8. What is the difference in length between these two lines?

Difference = _____ mm

9. What must be added to each amount to make 5 kg?

a)

1450 g + [   ] g

b)

2850 g + [   ] g

10. Complete these.

a) 5.9 litres = _____ ml

b) 8.65 litres = _____ ml

c) 3400 ml = _____ litres

d) 7250 ml = _____ litres

/10

Reading scales

1. What is the reading on each of these scales?

a)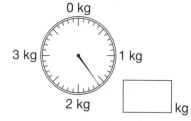

kg

b)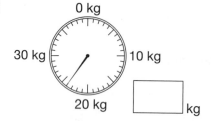

kg

2. Write each reading in millimetres.

a)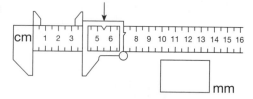

mm

b)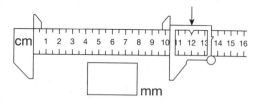

mm

3. How much liquid is in each jug? Write the amounts in millilitres.

a)

_____ ml

b)

_____ ml

4. Write these lengths in millimetres.

mm

mm

cm 1 2 3 4 5 6 7 8 9 10 11 12 13 14 15

5. What is the difference in length between the arrows in question 4?

Difference =   mm

6. 110 ml of liquid is added to this container. How much liquid will there be in total?

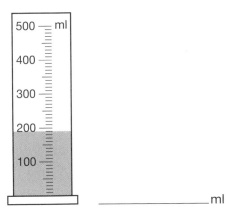

_____ml

7. What is the reading on each of these scales?

a)

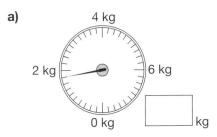

kg

b)

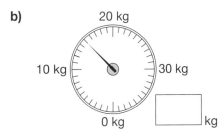

kg

8. What is the difference between the two readings in question 7? _____ kg

9. How much liquid is in each jug? Write the amounts in litres.

a)

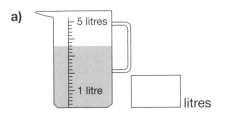

litres

b)

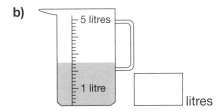

litres

10. 400 g of flour is taken off these scales.
What will the new reading be?

kg

/10

Perimeter

1. Draw a rectangle on this grid with a perimeter of 30 squares.

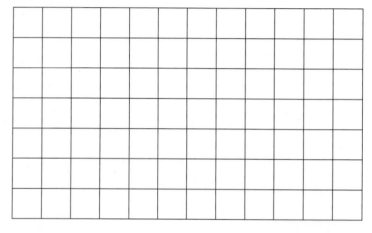

2. A square has sides of 35 mm each. What is the perimeter of the square?

_____mm

3. What is the perimeter of this rectangle?

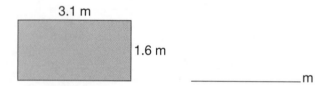

3.1 m

1.6 m

_____m

4. What is the perimeter of a regular pentagon with sides of 1.8 metres each?

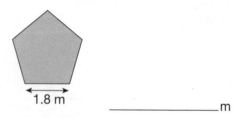

1.8 m

_____m

5. What is the perimeter of this shape?

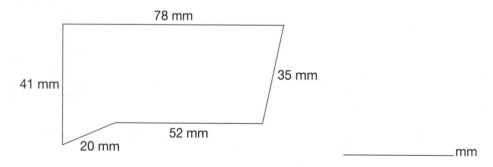

78 mm

41 mm

35 mm

20 mm

52 mm

_____mm

Perimeter

6. Draw two different shapes on this grid, each with a perimeter of 14 cm.

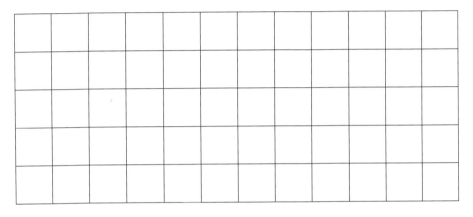

7. What is the perimeter of a square with an area of 81 cm²?

_____ cm

8. A rectangle has a perimeter of 64 mm. If the length of each of the longest sides is 21 mm, what is the length of each of the shortest sides?

_____ mm

9. What is the perimeter of this shape?

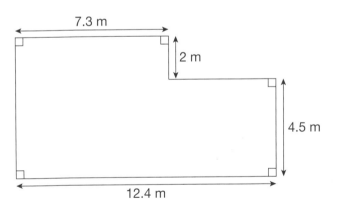

_____ m

10. What is the perimeter of an equilateral triangle in which each side measures 8.3 cm? Write your answer in millimetres.

_____ mm

/10

Area

1. What is the area of this rectangle?

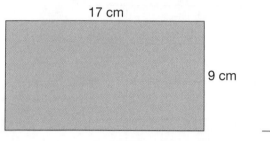

17 cm

9 cm

_____ cm²

2. Draw two different shapes on this grid, each with an area of 14 squares.

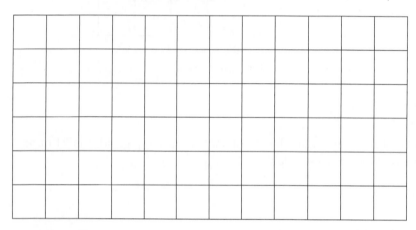

3. A square has a perimeter of 48 cm. What is the area of the square?

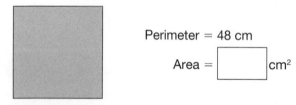

Perimeter = 48 cm

Area = ☐ cm²

4. A rectangle has an area of 96 cm². If one of the longer sides is 16 cm, what is the length of the shorter sides?

_____ cm

5. What is the area of this room?

12.5 m

6 m

_____ m²

Area

6. Draw a rectangle on this grid with an area of 24 cm².

7. A square has an area of 49 cm².
   What is the perimeter of the square?

   Area = 49 cm²

   Perimeter = _____ cm

8. This shape has two parts, A and B. What is the area of each part?

   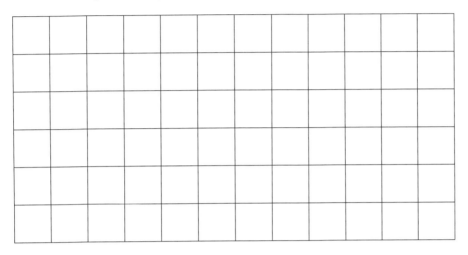

   a) Area of A = _____ cm²

   b) Area of B = _____ cm²

9. What is the total area of the shape, A + B, in question 8?

   Total area = _____ cm²

10. A rectangle has an area of 120 cm². If one of the longer sides is 15 cm, what is the length of the shorter sides?

   _____ cm

/10

Time

1. Write these as 24-hour clock times.

   a) 8 o'clock in the morning → _____

   b) 8 o'clock in the evening → _____

2. A train starts its journey at 13:50 and completes the journey 2 hours 30 minutes later.

   What time does the journey end? Write your answer as a 24-hour clock time.

   _____

3. Write these as 24-hour clock times.

   a)   a.m.   b)   a.m.   c)   p.m.

   [:]   [:]   [:]

4. Complete these.

   a) 1800 seconds = _____ minutes

   b) $10\frac{1}{2}$ minutes = _____ seconds

   c) $8\frac{1}{2}$ hours = _____ minutes

   d) 720 hours = _____ days

5. If the time is 11.38 a.m., what time will it be in $3\frac{1}{2}$ hours? Write your answer using a.m. or p.m.

   _____

6. Draw hands on the clocks to show these times.

a)
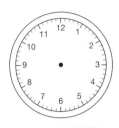

| 10 : 42 |

b)

| 14 : 08 |

c)

| 20 : 36 |

7. If today is Thursday 1st May, what date was it yesterday?

_____

8. Write these 24-hour clock times using a.m. or p.m.

a) 16:45 → _____

b) 11:53 → _____

c) 23:05 → _____

9. A train takes 1 hour 15 minutes between each stop. Complete the timetable.

Aston	10:42		
Bunstone		15:25	
Caleby	13:12		20:44

10. Write these times using the 24-hour clock.

a) 10.35 p.m. → _____

b) 8.49 a.m. → _____

c) 3.55 p.m. → _____

/10

Fraction calculations

1. What is the total of these two fractions?

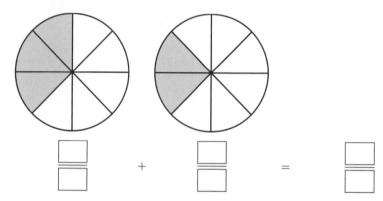

2. What is the difference between these two fractions?

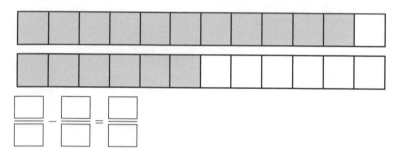

3. Colour the rectangle to show this addition.

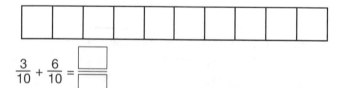

$\frac{3}{10} + \frac{6}{10} = $

4. $\frac{1}{2}$ of this bar of chocolate is eaten by Sam and then a further $\frac{1}{4}$ is broken off and eaten by Amy. How many squares of chocolate are left?

_____

Fraction calculations

5. Write the totals of these fractions in their simplest form.

a) $\frac{3}{5} + \frac{1}{5} = \boxed{}$

b) $\frac{3}{10} + \frac{2}{10} = \boxed{}$

c) $\frac{1}{2} + \frac{1}{4} = \boxed{}$

6. Colour the rectangle to show this addition.

$\frac{3}{4} + \frac{1}{8} = \boxed{}$

7. a) Answer this:

$\frac{7}{10} - \frac{3}{5} = \boxed{}$

b) Shade these rectangles to show the first two fractions of the sum in 7a.

8. Circle the missing fraction:

$\boxed{} + \frac{5}{6} = 1\frac{1}{6}$

$\frac{1}{6}$ $\frac{5}{6}$ $\frac{1}{2}$ $\frac{1}{3}$ $\frac{2}{3}$

9. A pizza is cut into 12 equal slices. Emma eats $\frac{1}{3}$ of it and Ali eats $\frac{1}{6}$ of it. How many slices are left?

_____

/10

10. Answer these, giving your answers in the simplest form:

a) $\frac{7}{10} - \frac{3}{10} = \boxed{}$

b) $\frac{11}{12} - \frac{7}{12} = \boxed{}$

c) $\frac{1}{2} - \frac{1}{4} = \boxed{}$

Tables, charts and graphs

This bar chart shows the maths test scores of a group of children. Use the information in the bar chart to answer the questions.

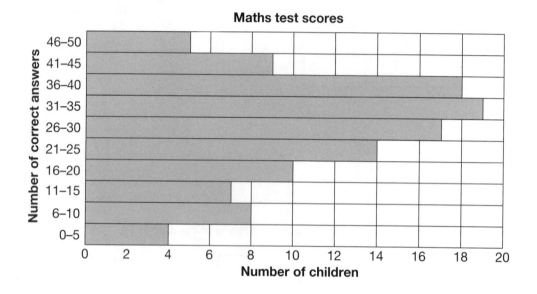

Maths test scores

1. How many children scored between 26 and 30 correct answers?

   _____

2. How many children scored between 46 and 50 correct answers?

   _____

3. How many children altogether scored more than 30 correct answers?

   _____

4. How many children altogether scored 20 or fewer correct answers?

   _____

5. What was the **mode** range of scores for this maths test?

   _____

Tables, charts and graphs

This graph shows the performance of a cyclist in a race.

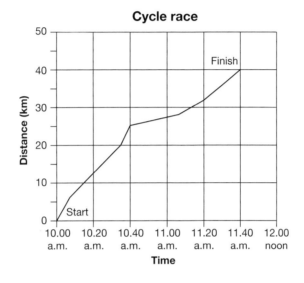

Cycle race

6. What time did the race start?

_____

7. How far had the cyclist travelled after 1 hour?

_____

8. At what time had the cyclist travelled 32 kilometres?

_____

9. What was the length of the race?

_____

10. How long did it take for the cyclist to complete the race?

_____

/10

Shape puzzle

Add one extra triangle to each shape to make it symmetrical.
Colour each shape to make symmetrical patterns.

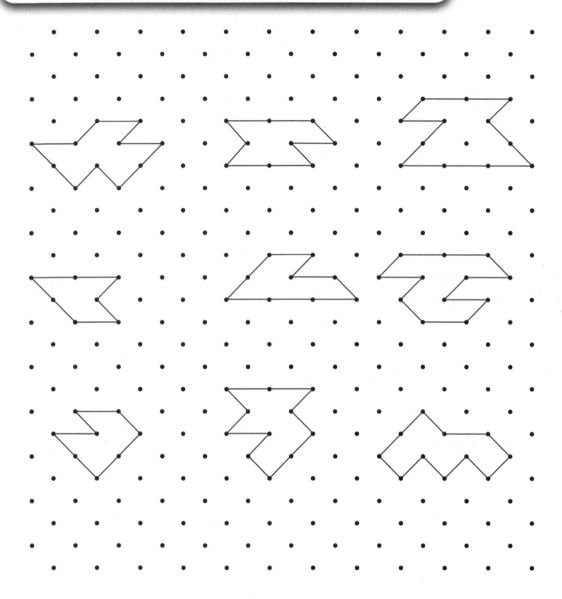

Maths maze

Move horizontally or vertically one number at a time through this maze to the finish. You can only move on to a number that is a multiple or factor of the number you are on.

Progress report

Record how many questions you got right and the date you completed each test.
This will help you to monitor your progress.

Test 1 /10 Date _____	**Test 2** /10 Date _____	**Test 3** /10 Date _____	**Test 4** /10 Date _____	**Test 5** /10 Date _____
Test 6 /10 Date _____	**Test 7** /10 Date _____	**Test 8** /10 Date _____	**Test 9** /10 Date _____	**Test 10** /10 Date _____
Test 11 /10 Date _____	**Test 12** /10 Date _____	**Test 13** /10 Date _____	**Test 14** /10 Date _____	**Test 15** If you got all of the missing numbers in less than 10 minutes, score yourself 10 marks. Date _____
Test 16 If you did this in less than 10 minutes, score yourself 10 marks. Date _____	**Test 17** /10 Date _____	**Test 18** /10 Date _____	**Test 19** /10 Date _____	**Test 20** /10 Date _____
Test 21 /10 Date _____	**Test 22** /10 Date _____	**Test 23** /10 Date _____	**Test 24** /10 Date _____	**Test 25** /10 Date _____
Test 26 /10 Date _____	**Test 27** /10 Date _____	**Test 28** /10 Date _____	**Test 29** If you complete all the shapes, score yourself 10 marks. Date _____	**Test 30** If you complete the maze, score yourself 10 marks. Date _____

Answers: Maths 10-Minute Tests, age 9–10

Test 1
1. 107   118   129
2. 8 -16 -22
3. **a)** -2 **b)** -11
4. $-4°C$
5. $2°C$
6. -8 1   7
7. **a)** -13 **b)** -4
8. $-2°C$
9. $-7°C$
10. 10 -6 -14

Test 2
1. 6.45 → $6\frac{45}{100}$
   6.5 → $6\frac{5}{10}$
   4.65 → $4\frac{65}{100}$
   5.6 → $5\frac{6}{10}$
   6.54 → $6\frac{54}{100}$
2. 6.1   6.5   7.2   7.8
3. **a)** 0.34   **b)** 0.19   **c)** 0.07
4. **a)** $\frac{51}{100}$ **b)** $\frac{92}{100}$ **c)** $\frac{8}{100}$
5. **a)** 3.84   **b)** 5.12   **c)** 4.29
6. 3.251 3.254 3.257 3.263 3.266
7. **a)** 9 tenths
   b) 8 thousandths
   c) 5 hundredths
8. **a)** 0.001   **b)** 0.021   **c)** 0.9
9. 486.795
10. **a)** $6\frac{249}{1000}$ **b)** $3\frac{21}{1000}$ **c)** $7\frac{555}{1000}$

Test 3
1. **a)** $20\,056 < 20\,506$
   b) $39\,989 > 39\,898$
2. **a)** 745.5   **b)** 36.85
   c) 1270.03
3. 29 906   29 945   208 865
   208 956   290 030
4. 30.19 kg
5. **a)** $0.011 < 0.111$
   b) $0.42 > 0.402$
   c) $0.658 > 0.568$
6. $-7°C$ $-1°C$
7. 37.45 m   37.5 m   37.91 m
   38.3 m   38.33 m
8. £74.88   £60.90   £40.05
   £38.70   £31.29
9. **a)** 7500   **b)** 25 000
10. $-20°C$ $-19°C$ $-17°C$
    $-11°C$ $0°C$ $3°C$

Test 4
1. 6535 → 6540
   6575 → 6580
   6548 → 6550
   6556 → 6560
   6573 → 6570
2. **a)** 17 000
   b) 30 000
   c) 50 000
3. **a)** £18
   b) £28
   c) £50

4. Any two numbers from
   11.5 to 12.49
5. **a)** 100 g   **b)** 200 g   **c)** 400 g
6. 1800 ml
7. **a)** 400   **b)** 200
8. **a)** 1770   **b)** 1320
9. 52.83 → 53
   52.08 → 52
   55.19 → 55
   53.51 → 54
10. 600–700 hours (696 hours)

Test 5
1. **a)** $\frac{11}{4}$ **b)** $\frac{4}{3}$
2. **a)** $4\frac{1}{2}$ **b)** $3\frac{3}{4}$
   c) $3\frac{3}{5}$ **d)** $6\frac{2}{3}$
3.

Fractions	Decimals	Percentages
$\frac{1}{2}$	0.5	50%
$\frac{1}{5}$	0.2	20%
$\frac{3}{4}$	0.75	75%
$\frac{3}{10}$	0.3	30%

4. 65%
5. **a)** 35%   **b)** 25%   **c)** 80%
6.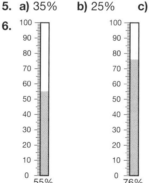
   55%   76%
7. $\frac{1}{5}$ → 0.2 → 20%
   $\frac{3}{10}$ → 0.3 → 30%
   $\frac{45}{100}$ → 0.45 → 45%
   $\frac{4}{5}$ → 0.8 → 80%
8. **a)** $\frac{90}{100}$ or $\frac{9}{10}$
   b) $\frac{5}{100}$ or $\frac{1}{20}$
   c) $\frac{60}{100}$ or $\frac{3}{5}$ or $\frac{6}{10}$
9. **a)** $0.8 > 8\%$ **b)** $0.2 < 50\%$
   c) $0.25 < 75\%$
10. **a)** $\frac{19}{4}$ **b)** $\frac{5}{2}$ **c)** $\frac{17}{3}$

Test 6
1. **a)** $\frac{4}{10} = \frac{2}{5}$ **b)** $\frac{3}{5} = \frac{6}{10}$
2. **a)** $\frac{14}{16}$ **b)** $\frac{12}{25}$
3. $\frac{2}{5} = \frac{4}{10} = \frac{6}{15} = \frac{8}{20} = \frac{10}{25}$
4. $\frac{5}{8}$
5. **a)** $\frac{3}{10} = \frac{15}{50}$ **b)** $\frac{5}{6} = \frac{15}{18}$
   c) $\frac{2}{3} = \frac{40}{60}$

6.
7. $\frac{6}{8} = \frac{3}{4}$
8. $\frac{5}{8} = \frac{10}{16} = \frac{15}{24} = \frac{20}{32} = \frac{25}{40}$
9. **a)** $\frac{2}{5}$ **b)** $\frac{1}{4}$ **c)** $\frac{7}{8}$
10. Check that the fractions are
    equivalent to $\frac{3}{5}$,
    e.g. $\frac{6}{10}, \frac{9}{15}, \frac{12}{20}, \frac{15}{25}$

Test 7
1. 3 red and 9 blue tiles
2. 3 green and 12 yellow tiles
3. 6 black and 10 white tiles
4. 200 g
5. $\frac{1}{3}$
6. $\frac{3}{5}$
7. 200 g fish
   500 g potatoes
   100 g peas
   80 g cheese
   40 g butter
   60 ml milk
8. 1 to 2 or 1 : 2
9. 16
10. 3 to 4 or 3 : 4

Test 8
1. **a)** 8   **b)** 6   **c)** 8
2. **a)**

×	7	9	6
8	56	72	48
7	49	63	42
4	28	36	24

   b)

×	10	11	12
8	80	88	96
9	90	99	108
10	100	110	120

3. **a)** 9   **b)** 7   **c)** 8
4. 24 and 48
5. $25 \div 3$ → r1
   $44 \div 5$ → r4
   $68 \div 9$ → r5
   $51 \div 8$ → r3
   $44 \div 6$ → r2
6. 36 → Any two from 2×18,
   3×12, 4×9
   60 → Any two from 2×30,
   3×20, 4×15, 5×12,
   6×10
   40 → Any two from 2×20,
   4×10, 5×8
   72 → Any two from 2×36,
   3×24, 4×18, 6×12,
   8×9

7. a)

×	9	5	6
3	27	15	18
8	72	40	48
7	63	35	42

b)

×	7	4	8
8	56	32	64
9	63	36	72
3	21	12	24

8. a) 6 b) 50 c) 7
9. 30
10. 4

Test 9
1. a) 1, 2, 4, 8, 16, 32
   b) 1, 2, 4, 5, 10, 20
   c) 1, 5, 25
   d) 1, 5, 11, 55
2. a) 20.
   b) 18.
   c) 36.
3. a) 12, 24, 36   b) 15, 30, 45
4. a) (1, 28) (2, 14) (4, 7)
   b) (1, 45) (3, 15) (5, 9)
   c) (1, 40) (2, 20) (4, 10) (5, 8)
   d) (1, 24) (2, 12) (3, 8) (4, 6)
5. True
6. 30, 45, 60
7. 45, 27
8. 60
9. a) 70   b) 48
10. True. Because it has no factors except for 1 and itself.

Test 10
1. a) 161 b) 216 c) 218
2. 1175 and 3825
   3281 and 1719
   2386 and 2614
   2208 and 2792
3. a) 6311   b) 4367
   c) 9423   d) 11641
4. 20.2 cm
5.

7.2	9.1	16.3
6.4	8.9	15.3
13.6	18	31.6

6. a) 46744 b) 69190 c) 78651
7. £56.44
8. a) 8315 + 1562 = 9877
   b) 4829 + 3152 = 7981
   c) 4229 + 2793 = 7022
9. £18.75 → £11.25
   £19.75 → £10.25
   £12.55 → £17.45
   £15.85 → £14.15
10. 349 + 76 = 425

Test 11
1. 154 → 66
   127 → 39
   134 → 46
   119 → 31
2. a) 1667   b) 2819   c) 2288
3. a) £6.42 b) £1.73 c) £3.91
4. a) 381 – 149 = 232
   b) 478 – 293 = 185
   c) 604 – 375 = 229
5. 344
6. 1289 km
7. 571 km
8. a) 42272 b) 20908 c) 26838
9. a) 5.58 litres   b) 4.37 litres
10. 1.35 metres

Test 12
1. a) 632   b) 370   c) 518
2.

IN	6	7	3	5	9
OUT	480	560	240	400	720

3. $57 \times 6 (= 342)$
4. a) 954   b) 2992
5. £20.88
6. a) 1862   b) 1482
7. a) 204 cm^2 b) 437 cm^2
8. 420 kg
9. a) 10992 b) 19254 c) 21912
10. 8075

Test 13
1. a) 16 r 3
   b) 35 r 1
2. a) 120
   b) 57
3.

IN	490	370	245	681	705
OUT	4.9	3.7	2.45	6.81	7.05

4. a) 64   b) 59   c) 113
5. 143   206   316
6. a) 81 b) 95 c) 66 d) 76
7. a) 1343 r 3
   b) 576 r 1
   c) 503
8. a) $5\overline{)749}$ = 149 r 4   b) $8\overline{)285}$ = 35 r 5
   c) $9\overline{)537}$ = 59 r 6
9. 97
10. 2

Test 14
1. a) $\frac{3}{5}$ of...   b) $\frac{2}{3}$ of...

   25 → 15   24 → 16
   40 → 24   30 → 20
   50 → 30   42 → 28
   65 → 39   90 → 60
2. a) 20p b) £5 c) £2
3. a) 90%   b) 90%
4. $\frac{4}{9}$

5. a) 39 kg   b) 450 ml
   c) 675 g   d) 90 cm
6. flour 240 g
   butter 160 g
   sugar 80 g
   raisins 200 g
   cherries 80 g
   walnuts 40 g
7. a) £7.50
   b) £15
   c) £3.75
   d) £11.25
8. $\frac{1}{6}$
9. $\frac{4}{7}$ of 63 litres
10. a) 4 kg   b) 1.5 kg   c) 7 kg

Test 15
1.

5	+	3	=	8
+		–		–
3	+	0	=	3
=		=		=
8	–	3	=	5

2.

4	+	4	=	8
+		×		–
5	+	2	=	7
=		=		=
9	–	8	=	1

3.

4	+	6	=	10
×		÷		–
3	×	2	=	6
=		=		=
12	÷	3	=	4

4.

12	÷	6	=	2
–		÷		×
8	–	2	=	6
=		=		=
4	×	3	=	12

5.

24	÷	6	=	4
÷		×		×
12	÷	2	=	6
=		=		=
2	×	12	=	24

6.

6	×	6	=	36
×		÷		÷
1	×	6	=	6
=		=		=
6	×	1	=	6

Test 16

1.

2.

3.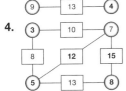

4.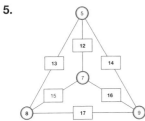

5.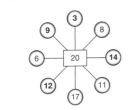

6.

Test 17

1.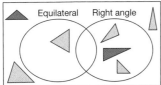
pentagon hexagon
octagon heptagon

2.

	A	B	C	D	E	F	G	H
Equilateral	✓				✓			✓
Isosceles		✓	✓	✓		✓	✓	

3. B and G
4. always true
5. rhombus
6.

Equilateral   Right angle

7. Check that a parallelogram or rhombus has been drawn.
8. sometimes true
9. 2nd, 4th and 5th shapes should be ticked.
10. A vertical line should be drawn from C (at right angles to line AB).

Test 18

1.

	A	B	C	D	E	F	G
Prisms	✓	✓			✓		
Pyramids			✓	✓	✓		✓

2. 6 faces, 12 edges and 8 vertices
3. a) triangular pyramid or tetrahedron
   b) triangular prism
4. sometimes true
5. 6
6. The 5th shape should be ticked.
7. 6
8. a) square-based pyramid
   b) pentagonal prism
9. cylinder
10. a) Check that a prism has been drawn.
   b) Check that a pyramid has been drawn.

Test 19

1. rectangle ➔ (2, 3)
2. pentagon ➔ (5, 8)
3. square ➔ (1, 7)
4. triangle ➔ (7, 5)
5. circle ➔ (4, 1)
6.   **7.**
8.   **9.**
10.

Test 20

1. a) 11 **b)** 19 **c)** 21
2. a) XVII **b)** XXIV **c)** XXIX
3.

4. a) XXXII > XXIV **b)** LXIII < LXX
5. True. Because X = 10 and C = 100. 100 − 10 = 90.
6. XLV L LIV LVIII LX
7. a) DXXXIV **b)** 534
8. 365 ➔ CCCLXV;
   356 ➔ CCCLVI; 536 ➔ DXXXVI;
   635 ➔ DCXXXV
9. DCCXXIV

10. 2015

Test 21

1.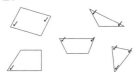

2. Check that an angle between 90° and 180° has been drawn.
3. a) 40° **b)** 110°
4. 360°
5. true
6. 65°
7. 180°
8. 270°
9. a) 60° **b)** 135° **c)** 80°
10. a) 60° **b)** 20° **c)** 55°

Test 22

1. a) 420 cm
   b) 6300 m
   c) 7.8 cm
   d) 0.8 m
2. 3.8 m
3. 850 g
4. 2.2 l
5. 7.9 cm = 79 mm
6. 5.15 km or 5150 m
7. a) 6700 g
   b) 3950 g
   c) 8.2 kg
   d) 4.75 kg
8. 15 mm
9. a) 3550 g
   b) 2150 g
10. a) 5900 ml
   b) 8650 ml
   c) 3.4 litres
   d) 7.25 litres

Test 23

1. a) 1.6 kg **b)** 24 kg
2. a) 55 mm **b)** 120 mm
3. a) 1400 ml **b)** 1900 ml
4. 25 mm 85 mm
5. 60 mm
6. 300 ml
7. a) 1.8 kg **b)** 15 kg
8. 13.2 kg
9. a) 3.6 litres **b)** 2.5 litres
10. 2.2 kg

Test 24

1. Check rectangle has a perimeter of 30 squares, e.g. 9 × 6.
2. 140 mm
3. 9.4 m
4. 9 m
5. 226 mm
6. Check both shapes have a perimeter of 14 cm.
7. 36 cm

8. 11 mm

9. 37.8 m

10. 249 mm

Test 25

1. 153 cm²

2. Check that the area of each shape is 14 squares.

3. 144 cm²

4. 6 cm

5. 75 m²

6. Check rectangle has an area of 24 cm², e.g. 12 cm × 2 cm, 8 cm × 3 cm, 6 cm × 4 cm.

7. 28 cm

8. a) 36 cm²
b) 12 cm²

9. 48 cm²

10. 8 cm

Test 26

1. a) 08:00
b) 20:00

2. 16:20

3. a) 08:55   **b)** 11:05   **c)** 14:25

4. a) 30 minutes
b) 630 seconds
c) 510 minutes
d) 30 days

5. 3.08 p.m.

6. a)
10 : 42

b)
14 : 08

c)
20 : 36

7. Wednesday 30th April

8. a) 4.45 p.m.
b) 11.53 a.m.
c) 11.05 p.m.

9.

Aston	10:42	**14:10**	**18:14**
Bunstone	**11:57**	15:25	**19:29**
Caleby	13:12	**16:40**	20:44

10. a) 22:35   **b)** 08:49   **c)** 15:55

Test 27

1. $\frac{3}{8} + \frac{2}{8} = \frac{5}{8}$

2. $\frac{11}{12} - \frac{6}{12} = \frac{5}{12}$

3. $\frac{9}{10}$

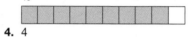

4. 4

5. a) $\frac{4}{5}$ **b)** $\frac{1}{2}$ **c)** $\frac{3}{4}$

6.

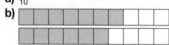

$\frac{7}{8}$

7. a) $\frac{1}{10}$

b)

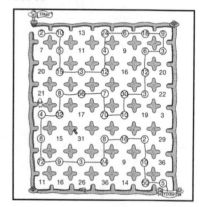

8. $\frac{1}{3}$

9. 6 slices

10. a) $\frac{2}{5}$ **b)** $\frac{1}{3}$ **c)** $\frac{1}{4}$

Test 28

1. 17

2. 5

3. 51

4. 29

5. 31–35 correct answers

6. 10.00 a.m.

7. 27 km (accept 28 km)

8. 11.20 a.m.

9. 40 km

10. 1 hour 40 minutes

Test 29

Check that the shapes have one extra triangle drawn to make each of them symmetrical.

Test 30

Alternative answers are possible.

KS2 Success

Age 9-10

Maths and English

10-Minute Tests

Paul Broadbent
and
Alison Head

Sample page

clear instructional text   topic being covered   test number for quick reference

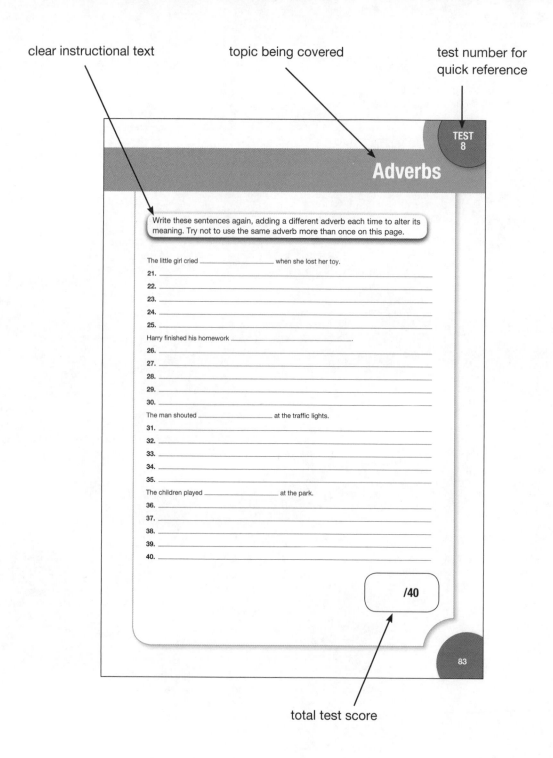

TEST
8

Adverbs

Write these sentences again, adding a different adverb each time to alter its meaning. Try not to use the same adverb more than once on this page.

The little girl cried _____ when she lost her toy.

21. _____
22. _____
23. _____
24. _____
25. _____

Harry finished his homework _____ .

26. _____
27. _____
28. _____
29. _____
30. _____

The man shouted _____ at the traffic lights.

31. _____
32. _____
33. _____
34. _____
35. _____

The children played _____ at the park.

36. _____
37. _____
38. _____
39. _____
40. _____

/40

83

total test score

Contents

Nouns

1–16. Sort the nouns in the box into the appropriate columns in the table below.

herd	Sally	Africa	fear	swarm	bravery
box	crowd	Amy	joy	table	
mountain	Wednesday	car	flock	excitement	

Common nouns	Proper nouns	Collective nouns	Abstract nouns

17–28. Now add three of your own nouns to each column.

Common nouns	Proper nouns	Collective nouns	Abstract nouns
17.	20.	23.	26.
18.	21.	24.	27.
19.	22.	25.	28.

Underline all of the nouns in each sentence.

29. Jane's happiness was written all over her face.

30. Max's understanding of symmetry is impressive.

31. The little girl's happy smile was lovely to see.

32. I took a bunch of flowers to school for Mrs Henry.

33. The man drove his car carefully through the snow.

34. London looked beautiful lit up in the moonlight.

35. I will always remember the man's kindness.

36. Last Friday, it rained all day.

37. A flock of geese flew over the river.

38. Carrie blew out the candles and made a wish.

Nouns

Write your own sentences using these nouns.

39. love _____

40. April _____

41. swarm _____

42. Friday _____

43. peace _____

44. company _____

45. examination _____

46. jealousy _____

47. holiday _____

48. chalk _____

49. floor _____

50. valley _____

/50

Silent letters

Underline the silent letter in each word.

1. knot

2. thumb

3. wrap

4. science

5. gnome

6. island

7. chalk

8. half

9. receipt

10. debt

11. ascend

12. autumn

13. biscuit

14. listen

15. chemist

Add the silent letter to complete each word.

16. anc__or

17. colum__

18. fei__n

19. dis__iple

20. campai__n

21. su__tle

22. c__orus

23. __noll

24. g__ess

25. __retched

26. this__le

Silent letters

27. g__ilty

28. crum__

29. C__ord

30. mis__ellaneous

> Underline the word in each sentence that contains a silent letter.

31. The choir sang a lovely song.

32. A sign warned us to stay off the grass.

33. I looked for a pair of scissors to cut the paper.

34. Amy knew all about fractions.

35. The cheers of the crowd echoed around the stadium.

36. The referee blew the whistle to end the match.

37. The divers explored the shipwreck.

38. Solomon takes guitar lessons every week.

39. Eve's design won the competition.

40. Our puppy loves to gnaw her rubber bone.

41. A silvery crescent moon hung in the sky.

42. Tim tried to guess what was in the package.

43. The class explored the ruins of a castle.

44. Billy hated combing his hair.

45. I saw the silhouette of the postman through the frosted glass.

46. Ashtsham wrote a brilliant story.

47. We found lots of interesting historical facts in the archive.

48. Grace was fascinated by the hot air balloon.

49. My little brother's birthday party was chaotic!

50. Soo completed a circuit of the running track in record time.

/50

ough letter string

Choose a word from the box that rhymes with each given word.

trough	rough	through	plough	thought	though

1. bluff _____

2. fort _____

3. cow _____

4. blue _____

5. below _____

6. off _____

Add the correct *ough* word to complete each sentence, using the clue letters to help you.

7. Simbo b_____ a new pair of shoes with her birthday money.

8. The jam d_____ left sugar all over my lips.

9. There was more than e_____ food for everyone at the picnic.

10. I t_____ I had finished all my homework.

11. The skin of the tomato was rather t_____.

12. The kittens f_____over the toy mouse.

13. Lucy had a sore throat and a nasty c_____.

14. The rare comic book was s_____ after by collectors.

15. "We _____t to be careful crossing the road," said Ben.

16. The animals crowded around the t_____ when the farmer
    b_____ their food.

17. A_____ it was late, Chris did not feel tired.

18. The b_____ of the tree was heavy with apples.

ough letter string

19. The farmer p―――――――――――――― the field, ready to sow the crops.

20. The baker kneaded the d――――――――――――.

> Write your own sentences using these *ough* words. Use a dictionary to help you if you get stuck.

21. drought

_____

22. breakthrough

_____

23. enough

_____

24. thoughtful

_____

25. nought

_____

26. brought

_____

27. roughly

_____

28. throughout

_____

29. thoroughly

_____

30. afterthought

_____

/30

-*ible* and -*able* words

Circle the correctly spelt word in each pair.

1. invisible   invisable
2. edable   edible
3. portible   portable
4. sensible   sensable
5. incredable   incredible
6. illegible   illegable
7. plausible   plausable
8. possable   possible
9. irresistible   irresistable
10. flexible   flexable
11. terrable   terrible
12. acceptable   acceptible
13. bearible   bearable
14. forgivable   forgivible
15. likeable   likeible
16. inflatible   inflatable
17. acceptible   acceptable
18. enjoyable   enjoyible
19. unbeatable   unbeatible
20. feasable   feasible

Add -*ible* or -*able* to complete these words.

21. tang_____
22. valu_____
23. suit_____
24. remov_____
25. gull_____
26. elig_____

-ible and *-able* words

27. divis_____   28. aud_____

29. notice_____   30. inescap_____

31. access_____   32. unforgett_____

33. horr_____   34. veget_____

35. sustain_____

Write a sentence using each of these words.

36. agreeable

_____

37. flexible

_____

38. achievable

_____

39. terrible

_____

40. responsible

_____

41. reversible

_____

42. washable

_____

43. remarkable

_____

44. irresistible

_____

45. reliable

_____

/45

Word roots

1–18. Colour in the words that share the same root. Use a different colour for each root.

act   government   operate   given   disapprove

cooperate   action   govern   pass   passenger

forgiveness   approval   prove   give

actor   passage   operator   governor

Write a word that shares the same **root** as each of these words. Do not use plural forms of the root word. Remember, to make your new word you can add either a **prefix** or a **suffix** to the root.

19. **child**hood   _____

20. **electric**ian   _____

21. **public**ity   _____

22. dis**cover**y   _____

23. **hero**ism   _____

24. **pain**killer   _____

25. **light**ning   _____

26. **pack**age   _____

27. en**joy**ment   _____

28. de**press**ion   _____

29. **hope**less   _____

30. mis**take**n   _____

Word roots

31. **usual**ly   _____

32. **develop**ing   _____

33. im**prison**ment   _____

34. ac**count**   _____

35. **favour**able   _____

36. **music**ian   _____

37. **assist**ance   _____

38. **agree**able   _____

39. **medic**ation   _____

40. re**call**   _____

41. **sign**al   _____

42. dis**interest**   _____

43. **infect**ious   _____

44. **clear**ance   _____

45. **disturb**ance   _____

46. **relax**ation   _____

47. **change**able   _____

48. **port**able   _____

49. **hand**icraft   _____

50. a**lone**   _____

/50

Using a thesaurus – synonyms

Use a thesaurus to find a word with a similar meaning for each of these words.

1. honest _____

2. huge _____

3. secret _____

4. crumple _____

5. hurry _____

6. ridicule _____

7. confused _____

8. fascinate _____

9. throw _____

10. disturb _____

11. agree _____

12. persist _____

13. increase _____

14. thrive _____

15. react _____

Using a thesaurus – synonyms

Write these sentences again, replacing the bold word with an alternative with a similar meaning. Use a thesaurus to help you if you need to.

16. The little dog was very **naughty.**

_____

17. There was a **cold** wind so I took a hat and gloves.

_____

18. The children **argued** about who should go first.

_____

19. The man struggled to **control** the large dog.

_____

20. Katie **wondered** how the book would end.

_____

21. Joe **planned** a day out with Ben.

_____

22. By the time we got home out clothes were **soaked** by the rain.

_____

23. Meg felt **sure** that she had passed her ballet exam.

_____

24. The football manager **refused** to comment on the result of the match.

_____

25. A **famous** author signed books at the library.

_____

/25

Verbs

Write the past tense of each verb.

1. walk _____
2. speak _____
3. go _____
4. wish _____
5. sleep _____
6. am _____
7. buy _____
8. weep _____
9. give _____
10. lose _____
11. worry _____
12. find _____
13. whisper _____
14. live _____
15. sweep _____
16. save _____
17. cry _____
18. leap _____
19. think _____
20. run _____

Underline the correct verb to complete each sentence.

21. It was freezing when we [wake waked woke] up.

22. I always [feel felt feeled] sick when I am in the car.

23. Jack [saves save saved] his money so he could buy a new game.

24. If Samia [tried try tries] hard in her test, she will get a good mark.

25. Katie [catched catch caught] chickenpox from her little brother last year.

26. Mrs Brown [teached teaches taught] me guitar when I get home from school.

27. Mum [works worked working] in a sweet shop when she was younger.

28. Our pumpkins [grow grew growed] so big that we could not lift them.

29. If Mum [knew knowed knows] I have lost my coat, she would be furious!

30. My cousins [come comed came] to my party last week.

Verbs

Write these sentences again in the past tense.

31. Lauren always wins running races.

_____

32. Sam plays football, even when it is raining.

_____

33. Nakia's school uniform is navy blue.

_____

34. Dad enjoys visiting Spain because he can speak Spanish.

_____

35. The boys tidy their rooms every Saturday morning.

_____

36. My sister makes a terrible mess when she is looking for something.

_____

37. We visit the castle during our holiday.

_____

38. Bhavin often leaves his schoolbag on the bus by mistake.

_____

39. I usually get to school on time.

_____

40. I read loads of books during the summer holidays.

_____

/40

Adverbs

Complete the table by turning the adjectives into adverbs. The first one has been done for you.

Adjective	Adverb
kind	kindly
1. brave	
2. hopeful	
3. rapid	
4. colourful	
5. nervous	
6. rude	
7. late	
8. sure	
9. angry	
10. dainty	

Underline the adverb in each sentence.

11. The children greedily gobbled up the cake.

12. Jake stared dreamily out of the window.

13. It will soon be time to go home.

14. The toddler wobbled unsteadily on her feet.

15. The school bell rang loudly to mark the end of the lesson.

16. Dad clapped proudly at the end of the play.

17. Leo finished his homework neatly so he would get top marks.

18. Suddenly, the wind blew the window open.

19. Almost every child passed the maths test.

20. Hundreds of stars twinkled brightly in the night sky.

Adverbs

Write these sentences again, adding a different adverb each time to alter its meaning. Try not to use the same adverb more than once on this page.

The little girl cried _____ when she lost her toy.

21. _____

22. _____

23. _____

24. _____

25. _____

Harry finished his homework _____.

26. _____

27. _____

28. _____

29. _____

30. _____

The man shouted _____ at the traffic lights.

31. _____

32. _____

33. _____

34. _____

35. _____

The children played _____ at the park.

36. _____

37. _____

38. _____

39. _____

40. _____

/40

More verbs

Underline the correct verb from the brackets to complete each sentence.

1. I [are am] too tired to finish my homework.

2. Rabbits [loves love] nibbling carrots.

3. "Why [was were] you late this morning?" asked Mr Malik.

4. Mum and Dad [watch watches] me play basketball every weekend.

5. Swallows [flies fly] south for the winter.

6. George always [laughs laugh] at the cartoons on TV.

7. Harmony [say says] she is coming to our house later.

8. I always [tries try] my best at school.

9. The boys [play plays] football in the back garden.

10. Eating fruit and vegetables [is are] good for you.

Add **is**, **are**, **was** or **were** to complete each sentence.

11. Claire _____ excited when she saw the pile of presents.

12. Anuja _____ going to a party this afternoon if she feels better.

13. We _____ the noisiest class in the school yesterday.

14. I will miss my friend because he _____ moving away.

15. Mum asked, "_____ you going to tidy your room today?"

16. Dad _____ angry when we broke the mirror.

17. Tom and Patrick _____ on their way here now.

18. Emily _____ afraid of the dark so she sleeps with a night light.

19. Dogs _____ great pets but they need a lot of attention.

20. We _____ just coming in when the telephone rang.

More verbs

Write these sentences again, correcting the verb errors.
Keep each sentence in the same tense as the original.

21. Do you know where Lisa were going?

_____

22. Is you looking forward to the theatre trip?

_____

23. Was you at ballet last week?

_____

24. The girls eats half of the pizza each.

_____

25. Robbie think he is the best writer in the class.

_____

26. My parents worries about us if we are late home.

_____

27. Mia's dog sleep on the end of her bed.

_____

28. Being active help to keep us healthy.

_____

29. Ben and Amy was sitting together in science.

_____

30. If I wins the prize, I will share it with you.

_____

/30

Using suffixes to make verbs

Complete these word sums. Remember, you sometimes need to remove a letter in order to complete the word sum.

1. dark + en = _____

2. formal + ise = _____

3. real + ise = _____

4. tight + en = _____

5. domestic + ate = _____

6. apology + ise = _____

7. pure + ify = _____

8. ripe + en = _____

9. note + ify = _____

10. public + ise = _____

11. replica + ate = _____

12. special + ise = _____

13. standard + ise = _____

14. medic + ate = _____

15. active + ate = _____

16. class + ify = _____

17. captive + ate = _____

18. glory + ify = _____

19. simple + ify = _____

20. awake + en = _____

Using suffixes to make verbs

Circle the correctly spelt word in each pair.

21. clearify   clarify

22. pacify   peacify

23. implycate   implicate

24. intenseify   intensify

25. beautify   beautyfy

26. memorise   memoryse

27. dramatise   dramaise

28. donorate   donate

29. televise   televisionise

30. liquefy   liquidify

Choose one of the suffixes from the box to add to each word.

-ate	-en	-ify	-ise

31. tight_____   32. advert_____

33. fix_____   34. final_____

35. sharp_____   36. hospital_____

37. acid_____   38. sign_____

39. moist_____   40. carbon_____

/40

Parentheses

Put a tick next to the sentences in which the brackets or dashes have been used correctly.

1. The Eiffel Tower built (in the centre of Paris) can be seen for miles around. ☐

2. The children (who were very tired) flopped lazily on the sofa. ☐

3. Her necklace – which was encrusted with diamonds – was priceless. ☐

4. Our summer holiday two weeks – on the island of Rhodes – was just the break we needed. ☐

5. Carl's moneybox (which contained all of his savings was very) heavy. ☐

6. The woodland (see map below) belongs to the local council. ☐

7. Our teacher was angry – absolutely furious, in fact – when he saw the messy classroom. ☐

8. There was party food (sausages rolls, crisps and tiny sandwiches) before the cake was brought out. ☐

9. Dad got up reluctantly – and headed for – the dancefloor. ☐

10. British Giant Rabbits can weigh more than 8 kg more than (17 lb)! ☐

Write the relevant part of each sentence again, adding the missing brackets or dashes to make the meaning clearer.

11. The football team (who had won their past four matches hoped to win the cup.

_____

12. My uncle is a funny man – he works in a circus after all but can still be quite strict.

_____

13. Our new classmate who has just arrived from Spain) sits next to Charlie.

_____

14. Rory said – and I heard him quite clearly that he would be home in time for dinner.

_____

Parentheses

15. The house (built when Queen Victoria was still on the throne had seen better days.

_____

16. I'm not happy about the playroom – my playroom being turned into a nursery for my baby brother.

_____

17. My sister who is hardly ever ill – is in bed with a bad cold.

_____

18. The author's latest book _When We Were Witches_ – is a best-seller.

_____

19. It rained all day and (as a result the cricket match was cancelled.

_____

20. I wore my thick coat (the one with the fur collar to stay warm in the snow.

_____

21. We iced the cake – the size of a pillow with bright pink frosting.

_____

22. Molly last year's fastest sprinter) is hoping to win the race.

_____

23. Daniel (Joe's twin is coming over for tea.

_____

24. Eve and her little dog) are always welcome.

_____

25. The man's car which was brand new – pulled into the car park.

_____

/25

Adverb fun

Find the list of adverbs hidden in the wordsearch grid.

surely	madly	hurriedly
solidly	calmly	totally
freshly	tidily	rudely
politely	messily	reluctantly
playfully	horribly	cheaply
painfully	quickly	happily
softly	heavily	

r	e	l	u	c	t	a	n	t	l	y	d	u	e	p	q	x
r	i	e	d	m	s	v	o	i	g	l	s	f	y	r	w	t
h	j	t	s	s	o	l	i	d	l	y	r	k	j	v	e	p
m	b	g	u	l	a	t	p	i	o	w	d	h	n	a	z	a
k	h	u	r	r	i	e	d	l	y	r	c	v	e	t	q	i
c	q	m	e	e	u	v	k	y	t	x	n	e	s	a	c	n
m	a	d	l	y	z	d	b	a	e	i	o	u	y	f	h	f
b	r	l	y	y	y	t	e	p	q	e	c	b	q	n	e	u
o	v	g	m	e	s	s	i	l	y	o	v	e	q	r	a	l
s	o	f	t	l	y	t	w	a	y	u	r	f	u	a	p	l
d	l	y	o	m	y	e	s	y	h	o	r	r	i	b	l	y
e	a	v	t	n	u	y	a	f	t	e	l	e	c	b	y	p
c	h	e	a	v	i	l	y	u	p	q	e	s	k	q	r	a
h	i	l	l	a	e	i	t	l	v	g	m	h	l	i	n	k
m	e	n	l	s	t	p	o	l	i	t	e	l	y	f	o	x
r	a	n	y	r	u	p	l	y	t	e	x	y	u	v	k	y
q	m	e	n	u	v	a	e	i	o	u	m	h	l	t	s	p
a	r	m	o	r	i	h	a	p	p	y	a	r	r	i	v	e

Modal verbs and adverbs of probability

Underline the adverb of probability in each sentence.

1. Perhaps we can have sausages for tea.

2. Maybe it will snow tonight.

3. He will definitely be at the party later.

4. Amy is certainly going to win the spelling prize.

5. Sports day will obviously be delayed if it rains.

6. Surely Ben will feel sick if he eats another cream cake!

7. They will doubtless be late because of the traffic.

8. Clare is the only one who could possibly beat Jamie at chess.

9. Simon is clearly the best person to play the lead in the show.

10. We will probably be at the zoo by lunchtime.

Write a sensible ending for these sentences, using the bold modal verb to help you.

11. If you go out in the rain you **will** _____.

12. Unless this traffic jam clears, I **shall** _____.

13. To do well at school you **should** _____.

14. When I get my pocket money I **might** _____.

15. In the winter it **can** _____.

16. The teacher came into the room before Bella **could** _____.

17. When the puppies are old enough they **may** _____.

18. Every morning on holiday we **would** _____.

19. When you are older you **can** _____.

20. If you forget the map you **might** _____.

/20

Direct and reported speech

Decide whether each sentence contains direct or reported speech.
Tick the correct box.

1. "Hurry up or we'll be late!" urged Mum. direct ☐ reported ☐

2. The little boy asked, "Can I have a balloon?" direct ☐ reported ☐

3. The teacher explained it would be playtime soon. direct ☐ reported ☐

4. "Let's play tennis," suggested Luke. direct ☐ reported ☐

5. The dentist told me my teeth were perfect. direct ☐ reported ☐

6. The old lady asked me to open the door for her. direct ☐ reported ☐

7. "Stop it!" snapped Kiera. direct ☐ reported ☐

8. "Would you like some more peas?" asked Dad. direct ☐ reported ☐

9. Rashid told me that he had finished his book. direct ☐ reported ☐

10. Susie complained that she was hungry. direct ☐ reported ☐

11. "It's snowing!" said Evie, excitedly. direct ☐ reported ☐

12. Greg muttered, "Go away!" direct ☐ reported ☐

13. Amy asked Chris if he felt better. direct ☐ reported ☐

14. "I'll see you later," said Dad, on his way out. direct ☐ reported ☐

15. Miss Morgan told the class to settle down. direct ☐ reported ☐

16. The little girl shouted, "I've won!" direct ☐ reported ☐

17. Sam complained that the work was hard. direct ☐ reported ☐

18. Max said he was learning to play chess. direct ☐ reported ☐

19. "It's time for bed," said Mum, firmly. direct ☐ reported ☐

20. "Is that a new top?" asked Mandy. direct ☐ reported ☐

Direct and reported speech

Write these sentences again, as reported speech.

Example: "I have arrived," said Fred.
Answer: Fred said he had arrived.

21. "Can we have a drink please?" asked the twins.

_____

22. "I love your picture Robbie," said Mr Parsons.

_____

23. "Get out of my room!" Maddie shouted at me.

_____

24. "I can't eat another thing!" said Dad, contentedly.

_____

25. "Have you seen the rainbow, Matthew?" asked Abdul.

_____

26. "I need to buy eggs and milk," said Mum.

_____

27. "Don't forget your packed lunch," Gran reminded me.

_____

28. The man asked, "What time does the train leave?"

_____

29. "Henry VIII had six wives," explained Mr Cooper.

_____

30. "I'd like a book of stamps please," asked the woman.

_____

/30

Dictionaries

Write these words in the order in which they appear in a dictionary.

1. gold, silver, platinum, brass, bronze

_____

2. grape, blueberry, banana, clementine, apple

_____

3. ten, two, thirty, twenty, thirteen

_____

4. lion, panther, leopard, lynx, jaguar

_____

5. beige, blue, black, brown, burgundy

_____

6. swallow, sparrow, starling, swift, swan

_____

7. cauliflower, carrot, cabbage, courgette, corn

_____

8. June, April, January, July, August

_____

9. sock, shirt, shoe, skirt, sweater

_____

10. angelfish, barracuda, anchovy, barfish, archerfish

_____

Write down a word that you could find between each of these words in a dictionary.

11. main _____ make

12. port _____ power

13. baby _____ band

14. fabric _____ feather

Dictionaries

15. trail _____ trampoline

16. caper _____ catch

17. rail _____ rare

18. ugly _____ under

19. acorn _____ again

20. beam _____ beat

21. daisy _____ dare

22. limb _____ lint

23. bulb _____ burn

24. climb _____ clip

25. dank _____ dawn

Look up these words in the dictionary and write a short definition.

26. irate _____

27. succinct _____

28. ambiguous _____

29. empathy _____

30. vagrant _____

31. aroma _____

32. precipice _____

33. altercation _____

34. oblivious _____

35. replicate _____

/35

Inference

> Read the sentences then answer the questions. You may need to continue your answers on a separate sheet.

1. Rachael tasted the soup, pulled a face and pushed the bowl away.

What did Rachael think of the soup and how do you know?

_____

_____

2. Seeing the score on his test paper, Will regretted spending the weekend playing football.

Why does Will regret playing football, and what does this have to do with his test paper?

_____

_____

3. Callum's mum finished reading his school report and flung it onto the kitchen table, fixing him with one of her fiercest looks.

What do you think Callum's report was like? How do you know?

_____

_____

4. Kerrie saw the lid of the cardboard box shift slightly and heard a soft mewing sound from inside.

What do you think was in the box and how do you know?

_____

_____

5. As the queue of traffic snaked slowly through the town, Dad drummed his fingers on the dashboard, sighed heavily and checked his watch again.

Why do you think Dad is behaving the way he is? How do you know?

_____

_____

Inference

6. **Feeling their way along the path, the boys were startled by an owl hooting invisibly nearby.**

   What time of day does the action in this sentence take place and how do you know?

   _____

   _____

7. **When she saw her friends approaching, Emma hastily tucked the bag of sweets into her pocket.**

   Why do you think Emma put her sweets away?

   _____

   _____

8. **When he saw his father approaching, Tommy's face lit up and he ran towards him.**

   How do you think Tommy feels about seeing his father and why does he run to him?

   _____

   _____

9. **As the woman got out of her car, she trembled and reluctantly went to have a look at the bumper.**

   What do you think might have happened?

   _____

   _____

10. **When Clara sneezed yet again, her mum sent her straight to bed.**

    Why do you think Clara was sent to bed?

    _____

    _____

/10

Homophones

Homophones are words that sound the same but have different meanings. Circle the correct word in the brackets to complete each sentence.

1. "Come [here hear]," said Mrs Ross.

2. We could [here hear] fireworks in the distance.

3. The boys packed away [there their] PE kits.

4. Will [there their] be time to play later?

5. The little girl was [to too] short to reach the high shelf.

6. We walk [to too] school with our friends.

7. We had a [grate great] time at the beach.

8. I had to [grate great] the cheese for the pizza.

9. Dad had to [brake break] hard when a cat ran into the road.

10. The boys will [brake break] the window if their ball hits it.

11. I am not [allowed aloud] to play outside when it is dark.

12. Paddy loves to read [allowed aloud] to the class.

13. Our teacher [lead led] us around the art gallery.

14. The church roof is covered in [lead led].

15. [Wear Where] are you going?

16. I am going to [where wear] my new dress to the party.

17. There are [eight ate] children going on the school trip.

18. My sister [eight ate] the last piece of cake.

19. We caught [sight site] of the white cliffs of Dover.

20. It is not safe to play on a building [sight site].

Homophones

Write your own sentences using these homophones.

21. weather _____

22. whether _____

23. weight _____

24. wait _____

25. meet _____

26. meat _____

27. no _____

28. know _____

29. waste _____

30. waist _____

31. eye _____

32. I _____

33. past _____

34. passed _____

35. by _____

36. buy _____

37. rode _____

38. road _____

39. their _____

40. there _____

/40

More suffixes

Circle the correctly spelled word in each group.

1.	mition	mission	mician
2.	magician	magitian	magission
3.	confution	confussion	confusion
4.	competition	competission	competician
5.	station	stacian	stasion
6.	pollucian	pollution	pollusion
7.	session	sesion	setion
8.	extention	extencian	extension
9.	optition	optician	optission
10.	explosion	explotion	explossion
11.	possetion	possession	possesion
12.	completion	complecian	complesion
13.	diction	dictian	dicsion
14.	profecian	profesion	profession
15.	emotion	emocian	emosion
16.	reducian	reducsion	reduction
17.	contribution	contribusion	contribucian
18.	mantion	manssion	mansion
19.	educasion	educacian	education
20.	proporsion	proporcian	proportion

Add **cian**, **sion**, **ssion** or **tion** to complete each word.

21. politi_____

22. exclu_____

23. fic_____

24. discu_____

25. devo_____

More suffixes

26. atten_____

27. lo_____

28. distribu_____

29. posi_____

30. founda_____

31. electri_____

32. direc_____

33. oppre_____

34. transfu_____

35. na_____

36. transla_____

37. repeti_____

38. frac_____

39. constitu_____

40. promo_____

41. peti_____

42. dele_____

43. occupa_____

44. infu_____

45. demonstra_____

46. intui_____

47. corro_____

48. mo_____

49. opposi_____

50. pa_____

/50

Relative clauses

Underline the relative clause in each sentence.

1. The children who live next door came round to play.

2. I was reading a book when the phone rang.

3. The ball that broke the window belongs to my brother.

4. All of the roads which lead into town were full of cars.

5. We live next door to a family whose pet rabbits keep escaping.

6. That is the house that we used to live in.

7. Who was that boy whom you were talking to?

8. That is the stadium where my favourite team plays.

9. I left some questions which were too difficult for me.

10. Chloe was surprised when her cousins knocked on the door.

11. The picture that won the art prize was amazing.

12. My older sister is a person whose bedroom is always tidy.

13. There was a huge puddle where we needed to cross the road.

14. The actor who starred in the new film is my favourite.

15. We were so cold when it began to snow.

Relative clauses

Write your own words to complete each sentence in a sensible way.

16. _____ whom we met at the park.

17. _____ when the party invitation arrived.

18. _____ where you can buy the best sweets.

19. _____ who always gets full marks in tests.

20. _____ whose car was blocking our driveway.

21. _____ which arrived at the station on time.

22. _____, which was full of teachers and parents.

23. _____, who was upset, _____.

24. _____, which were laden with apples, _____.

25. The children in 5F, whose _____,

_____.

26. _____ when I opened the parcel.

27. _____ that leads to my house.

28. _____ who wrote this book _____.

29. _____ whose dog was barking.

30. _____

/30

_____ who wrote me that email.

Adverbials of time, place and number

Circle the adverbial of number in these sentences.

1. To make a fruity milkshake, firstly you must choose your fruit.

2. Secondly, wash the fruit and place it in the blender with some vanilla ice cream.

3. Lastly, blend the ingredients together until smooth.

Choose the most appropriate adverbial of place from the brackets to complete the sentence.

4. We live two miles [nearby to from] the seaside.

5. The marina is four miles [away close over].

6. You can buy buckets and spades from a [far nearby down] shop.

Circle the adverbial of time in these sentences.

7. We usually go swimming on Saturdays.

8. My brother sometimes takes my things without asking.

9. I will meet you there later.

10. It was very hot yesterday.

Adverbials of time, place and number

Finish these sentences, using the adverbial to help you.

11. During the play _____.

12. In the summer I always _____.

13. We _____ all day.

14. _____ nearby.

15. I don't live far from _____.

16. _____ is far away.

17. Later, we will _____.

18. We climbed into _____.

19. Since I was a little child, _____.

20. Last week _____.

21. It is rarely _____.

22. Our teacher always _____.

23. Soon it will _____.

24. Next year, _____.

25. Since I have known my best friend, _____.

/25

Onomatopoeia

Onomatopoeia is where words sound like the things they describe. Write a noun you associate with each of these onomatopoeic words.

1. hiss _____

2. buzz _____

3. bang _____

4. pop _____

5. sizzle _____

6. drip _____

7. sniff _____

8. howl _____

9. chuckle _____

10. slither _____

11. whoosh _____

12. clatter _____

13. crunch _____

14. click _____

15. squelch _____

16. squeak _____

17. thud _____

18. creak _____

Write an onomatopoeic word to describe the sound that each of these things makes.

19. a parrot _____

20. a pile of tin cans falling over _____

Onomatopoeia

21. a bonfire   _____

22. stamping in a puddle   _____

23. speaking very quietly   _____

24. a twig breaking   _____

25. a window breaking   _____

26–35. Choose one of these themes and write a poem about it, using as much onomatopoeia as you can. Your poem should be at least 10 lines long. Before you start, you may find it useful to create a word bank of onomatopoeic words for your chosen theme on a separate piece of paper.

- a snake slithering through dry grass
- a storm at sea
- a fireworks display

_____

_____

_____

_____

_____

_____

_____

_____

_____

/35

Figurative language

Underline the alliteration in these sentences.

1. Tree boughs bobbed in the wind.

2. The crafty cat crawled towards the bird.

3. There was a spell of wet, windy weather.

4. The old gate was rust red.

5. My sister's sweet smile cheered me up.

6. Bobbie's balloon burst with a pop.

7. Maggie sank into the plump, purple pillow.

8. The creepy castle loomed over us.

9. Chris won a Super Student award.

10. Paula picked pink paint.

Write down whether each phrase is a simile or a metaphor.

11. The moon was a silver coin in the sky. _____

12. The field of corn rippled in the breeze like an ocean of gold. _____

13. A wave of excitement washed over her. _____

14. Anxiety gnawed at him like a dog with a bone. _____

15. The teacher's tone was as sharp as a tack. _____

16. The basketball player was as tall as a skyscraper. _____

17. My little cousin is as playful as a kitten. _____

18. The wet road was a black ribbon in the headlights. _____

19. A chilly draught crept through the keyhole like a thief. _____

20. The millpond was a mirror for the sky. _____

Write a phrase using personification for these things.

21. tree branches _____

22. a mountain _____

23. flowers in a breeze _____

24. waves lapping on a beach _____

25. windows of a deserted house _____

26. birds in the trees _____

27. the moon _____

28. time _____

29. the wind _____

/30

30. the sun _____

Fun with onomatopoeia

Unscramble the onomatopoeic words to complete the sentences.

1. ckelcra _____ like a bonfire

2. istwhle _____ like a referee

3. iffsn _____ if you have a cold

4. ralett _____ a kind of snake

5. macsk _____ like a ball hitting a wall

6. latcter _____ like a ladder falling over

7. ridp _____ like raindrops

8. shoohw _____ up like a rocket

9. pri _____ like paper

10. scrpea _____ like removing ice from a windscreen

11. shsi _____ like a snake

12. rkaec _____ like an old chair

13. lwho _____ like a wolf

14. lwia _____ like a baby

15. reltrsu _____ like autumn leaves

Pronouns

Underline the pronoun(s) in each sentence.

1. Our dog dug up the bone and ate it.

2. Maisie was late home, so Dad went out to look for her.

3. The restaurant served us delicious pizza.

4. Habib is great at scoring goals, but he isn't so good at goalkeeping.

5. The boys were cold when they came in from playing in the snow.

6. My sister and I can watch a film after we get back from school.

7. Mum tried to catch the spider, but it scuttled under the sofa.

8. Claire has two kittens and loves taking care of them.

9. The balloon popped because my nail was too sharp.

10. Tim's shoes were too tight, so Mum bought him some more.

Choose the best pronoun from the brackets to complete each sentence.

11. The children missed some of their playtime because _____ were being too noisy.
[it they us]

12. The cat saw a squirrel and chased _____ up a tree. [us her it]

13. I am going to Matthew's party, so I will buy _____ a present. [her us him]

14. My little brother is ill, so Dad took _____ to the doctor's. [him he you]

15. _____ love my bedroom because it has all my things in it. [He Her I]

16. My cousins can speak Spanish because _____ live in Spain.
[we they them]

17. The lady ran down the street because _____ needed to catch the bus.
[her he she]

18. My sister and I get into trouble if _____ don't keep our rooms tidy.
[we you it]

19. It is Mum's birthday, so Dad bought _____ some flowers. [her he them]

20. The people had lots of shopping, so the assistant fetched _____ a trolley.
[they them us]

Pronouns

Write these sentences again, replacing the bold words with a suitable pronoun.

21. Kate hurt her ankle when **Kate** slipped off the kerb.

_____

22. When the tree blew down **the tree** crushed our shed.

_____

23. Max and Robin shared a cake because **Max and Robin** could only afford one.

_____

24. When my family arrived at the restaurant, the waiter took **my family** to a table by the window.

_____

25. Molly is the best dancer in our class because **Molly** has been dancing for many years.

_____

26. Mr Welsh is a scary teacher because **Mr Welsh** shouts a lot.

_____

27. Jessica and I were late for school because **Jessica and I** took a wrong turning.

_____

28. Uncle Pete took the TV back to the shop because **the TV** did not work.

_____

29. Robert caught a crab after Mum showed **Robert** how to.

_____

30. The children were fed up because **the children** were tired of queuing for the ride.

_____

/30

Verb prefixes

Choose one of the prefixes from the brackets to add to each
word, then write the new word on the line provided.

1. [over re dis]direct _____

2. [dis un de]code _____

3. [over re dis]fund _____

4. [de over dis]look _____

5. [dis mis de]appear _____

6. [de over dis]heat _____

7. [dis over mis]interpret _____

8. [de mis over]inform _____

9. [mis de dis]port _____

10. [dis de over]agree _____

11. [mis de dis]able _____

12. [re de dis]print _____

13. [over de dis]believe _____

14. [mis re de]unite _____

15. [re dis over]call _____

Verb prefixes

Write your own sentences using these words.

16. disobeyed _____

17. misunderstand _____

18. overtake _____

19. disapprove _____

20. overload _____

21. defrost _____

22. misbehave _____

23. discourage _____

24. overcharge _____

25. disappointed _____

26. disconnect _____

27. misplaced _____

28. react _____

29. overcome _____

30. rebuild _____

/30

More pronouns

Underline the possessive pronoun in each sentence.

1. Those books are mine.

2. I love that bike but it is his.

3. Their project is good but ours is better.

4. "Are those trainers yours?" asked Lewis.

5. The school's computers are brand new but ours are much older.

6. The games belong to me but the console is theirs.

7. Scott said the bag was his.

8. Tom's test score was good but yours is excellent.

9. Those sweets are theirs so we must not eat them.

10. All of the books on that shelf are mine.

11. Saira's phone was ringing but I did not answer it because it was hers.

12. Although the cake was his, Peter shared it with the class.

13. The opposing team's competition entry is good, but I hope ours is better.

14. Milly was annoyed that we had tried the chocolates because they were hers.

15. Dad loves the car he has just bought but Mum thinks hers is better.

More pronouns

Circle the relative pronoun in these sentences.

16. The bus that stops at the end of our street was late.

17. My great-grandmother, who is ninety three, still loves to dance.

18. We had pizza for tea, which is my favourite.

19. This is Georgia, whom you met at my birthday party.

20. The person who knocked on the door was our neighbour, Mr Briggs.

21. The car that sped past was bright red.

22. My aunt, whom I like very much, is coming to visit next week.

23. Our teacher, who is very kind, is called Mrs Clarke.

24. The shop did not have the magazine that I wanted.

25. The child whose school book is neatest will win a prize.

26. The dog that is barking lives down the street.

27. The hat, which is blue, matches the gloves perfectly.

28. The team that scores the most goals will win the cup.

29. Tim is the one who baked the cake.

30. The bird that swooped out of hedge startled me.

/30

Writing speech

Decide whether each sentence has the correct speech punctuation, then put a tick or a cross in the box at the end.

1. "It's time to tidy up your things," reminded Mum. ☐

2. "Dad complained, the car won't start." ☐

3. Can I get you some drinks? "asked the waitress." ☐

4. Bobby asked, "Why is the sky blue?" ☐

5. "Your tickets are booked now," confirmed the lady. ☐

6. "How about checking your spelling?" suggested Claire. ☐

7. "What were you doing" in the hall? demanded Mr Turner. ☐

8. "Don't worry. It will be fine," comforted Grandma. ☐

9. "Come" in, said Auntie Beth, opening the door. ☐

10. "Go away!" snapped my sister, "rudely." ☐

Add the speech punctuation to these sentences.

11. Don't wake Dad, whispered Mum.

12. When will it stop raining? wondered Jack.

13. This isn't the one I wanted! complained the man.

14. You're wrong! argued Sophie.

15. The teacher explained, You need to measure carefully.

16. Is this platform four? queried the woman.

17. Dad insisted, You must eat your vegetables.

18. Have you seen her dress? gossiped the girls.

19. Will giggled, That's so funny!

20. I'm thirsty, grumbled Elsa.

Writing speech

Add an alternative to "said" to each sentence. Use the ideas in questions 1–20 in this test if you get stuck and try not to use the same word more than once.

21. "David kicked me under the table!" _____ Robert.

22. "Can I tell you a secret?" _____ Fiona.

23. "There's a spider!" _____ Rachel.

24. Callum _____, "Is there any more pizza?"

25. "I've won!" _____ Mum.

26. Jane _____, "Is the train on time?"

27. Joe _____, "That's not fair!"

28. "Light travels faster than sound," _____ Mr Fitz.

29. "I hope your brother will be OK," _____ Mum.

30. The man _____, "This soup is cold."

31–40. Write your own conversation between two characters. Use the correct speech punctuation and avoid using the word "said" where possible.

_____

_____

_____

_____

_____

_____

_____

_____

/40

Apostrophes

Put a tick or a cross in the box to show whether the possessive apostrophe is in the correct place.

1. A girl's story won the competition. ☐

2. The boys' toe was broken during the football match. ☐

3. The mens' briefcases were lined up on the train. ☐

4. The dogs' tail wagged frantically when he saw us. ☐

5. My hamster's fur feels soft when you stroke her. ☐

6. Brionys' hair is really long. ☐

7. My favourite book's pages were creased and torn. ☐

8. A squirrel's tail is long and bushy. ☐

9. Most cities' roads are very busy during rush hour. ☐

10. Three babies' prams were parked outside the shop. ☐

Add the possessive apostrophe to each sentence.

11. A trains passengers were forced to wait when it broke down.

12. The childrens coats were hung up neatly in the cloakroom.

13. Many students pictures were displayed on the wall.

14. Auntie Pats car is bright pink.

15. The pigeons heads bobbed back and forth as they walked about.

16. In my picture, all of the fairies wings are sparkly.

17. The queens crown was covered in diamonds.

18. The girls noses were bright pink when they came in from the cold.

19. The little boys shoes were on the wrong feet.

20. A dogs sense of smell is very good.

Apostrophes

Write the contracted forms of these phrases

21. could not _____.

22. I am _____.

23. she is _____.

24. they are _____.

25. we have _____.

26. shall not _____.

27. will not _____.

28. should have _____.

29. it is _____.

30. you will _____.

/30

Adjectives

Add a suitable adjective to each sentence.

1. A _____ butterfly fluttered from rose to rose.

2. The _____ kitten played with a ball of string.

3. We baked a _____ cake at school.

4. _____ snowflakes drifted to the ground.

5. A _____ boy rang the doorbell then ran away.

6. We organised a _____ birthday party for Sam.

7. Chloe was my _____ friend at school.

8. The toffee was _____ and _____ .

9. A _____ , _____ kite bobbed in the sky.

10. The _____ boy scored full marks in the test.

Complete the table of comparative and superlative adjectives.

Adjective	+er	+est
11–12. small		
13–14. kind		
15–16. brave		
17–18. big		
19–20. bright		
21–22. lovely		
23–24. funny		
25–26. rude		
27–28. fit		
29–30. young		

Adjectives

31–40. Add suitable adjectives to this piece of text to create a spooky mood.

Connor walked cautiously up the _____ pathway towards the house. _____ windows stared down at him, framed by _____ wooden shutters. He tried the _____ door, which creaked open on _____ hinges.

Inside, the house was totally _____. _____ curtains hung at the windows and cobwebs covered the _____ wallpaper. A crooked flight of stairs led up into _____ darkness. Connor was _____.

41–50. Write your own description of a theme park, using ten powerful adjectives.

_____

_____

_____

_____

_____

_____

_____

_____

_____

_____

/50

Connectives

Underline the connectives in these sentences.

1. The vase is broken because I dropped it.

2. The boys grabbed their bags and headed for school.

3. Although she was tired, Mum finished the ironing.

4. Mark was late, so he took the bus.

5. Mum went shopping while Dad took us to the cinema.

6. Because the car broke down, we had to call a taxi.

7. So he would remember his book, Sudip left himself a note.

8. After they had eaten their lunch, the children went outside to play.

9. I wanted to stay up late until the programme had finished.

10. We went to visit our aunt, but she was not in.

Add the most suitable connective from the brackets to complete each sentence.

11. I am having a party _____ it is my birthday. [although so because]

12. I read to Dad _____ he was cooking dinner. [during while and]

13. Erin picked up the books _____ arranged them on the shelf. [and so but]

14. The sun was shining, _____ we played in the garden. [however although so]

15. Jayden shared his lunch _____ he was hungry. [because although but]

16. Gemma likes netball _____ Marie prefers gymnastics. [so because but]

17. The teacher was pleased _____ the class had worked well. [and so because]

18. _____ it was raining, the laundry got wet. [So Although Because]

19. _____ her headache, Leah went to drama club. [Despite Although Because]

20. _____ crossing the road, the girls looked carefully both ways. [After Before And]

Connectives

Write each pair of sentences again as one sentence, replacing the full stop with a suitable connective.

21. It was windy. A tree blew down.

_____

22. We missed the bus. We had to wait for the next one.

_____

23. I looked for my phone. It was under my bed.

_____

24. We clapped and cheered. Our team scored a goal.

_____

25. We looked at the stars. Night fell.

_____

26. I wanted strawberry ice-cream. The shop only had vanilla.

_____

27. Joe entered the competition. He won!

_____

28. It was not raining. The sky was full of black clouds.

_____

29. The woman sat down for a rest. Her shopping bags were heavy.

_____

30. I told her the secret. I trusted her.

_____

/30

Progress report

Record how many questions you got right and the date you completed each test.
This will help you to monitor your progress.

Test 1 **/50** Date _____	**Test 2** **/50** Date _____	**Test 3** **/30** Date _____	**Test 4** **/45** Date _____	**Test 5** **/50** Date _____
Test 6 **/25** Date _____	**Test 7** **/40** Date _____	**Test 8** **/40** Date _____	**Test 9** **/30** Date _____	**Test 10** **/40** Date _____
Test 11 **/25** Date _____	**Test 12** Did you find all of the words? If you did it in less than 10 minutes, score yourself 20 marks. Date _____	**Test 13** **/20** Date _____	**Test 14** **/30** Date _____	**Test 15** **/35** Date _____
Test 16 **/10** Date _____	**Test 17** **/40** Date _____	**Test 18** **/50** Date _____	**Test 19** **/30** Date _____	**Test 20** **/25** Date _____
Test 21 **/35** Date _____	**Test 22** **/30** Date _____	**Test 23** If you completed this in less than 10 minutes, score yourself 10 marks. Date _____	**Test 24** **/30** Date _____	**Test 25** **/30** Date _____
Test 26 **/30** Date _____	**Test 27** **/40** Date _____	**Test 28** **/30** Date _____	**Test 29** **/50** Date _____	**Test 30** **/30** Date _____

Answers: English 10-Minute Tests, age 9–10

Test 1
1–16.

Common nouns	Proper nouns	Collective nouns	Abstract nouns
box	Sally	herd	fear
mountain	Africa	swarm	bravery
table	Amy	crowd	joy
car	Wednesday	flock	excitement

17–28. Answers will vary.
29. Jane's happiness was written all over her face.
30. Max's understanding of symmetry is impressive.
31. The little girl's happy smile was lovely to see.
32. I took a bunch of flowers to school for Mrs Henry.
33. The man drove his car carefully through the snow.
34. London looked beautiful lit up in the moonlight.
35. I will always remember the man's kindness.
36. Last Friday it rained all day.
37. A flock of geese flew over the river.
38. Carrie blew out the candles and made a wish.
39–50. Sentences will vary.

Test 2
1. knot
2. thumb
3. wrap
4. science
5. gnome
6. island
7. chalk
8. half
9. receipt
10. debt
11. ascend
12. autumn
13. biscuit
14. listen
15. chemist
16. anchor
17. column
18. feign
19. disciple
20. campaign
21. subtle
22. chorus
23. knoll
24. guess
25. wretched
26. thistle
27. guilty
28. crumb
29. chord
30. miscellaneous
31. choir
32. sign
33. scissors
34. knew
35. echoed
36. whistle
37. shipwreck
38. guitar
39. design
40. gnaw
41. crescent
42. guess
43. castle
44. combing
45. silhouette
46. wrote
47. archive
48. fascinated
49. chaotic
50. circuit

Test 3
1. rough
2. thought
3. plough
4. through
5. though
6. trough
7. bought
8. doughnut
9. enough
10. thought
11. tough
12. fought
13. cough
14. sought
15. ought
16. trough brought
17. Although
18. bough
19. ploughed
20. dough

Test 4
1. invisible
2. edible
3. portable
4. sensible
5. incredible
6. illegible
7. plausible
8. possible
9. irresistible
10. flexible
11. terrible
12. acceptable
13. bearable
14. forgivable
15. likeable
16. inflatable
17. acceptable
18. enjoyable
19. unbeatable
20. feasible
21. tangible
22. valuable
23. suitable
24. removable
25. gullible
26. eligible
27. divisible
28. audible
29. noticeable
30. inescapable
31. accessible
32. unforgettable
33. horrible
34. vegetable
35. sustainable
36–45. Possible answers include:
36. The cake has a very agreeable flavour.
37. The ruler was flexible so it did not break.
38. Winning the contest seemed like an achievable goal.
39. The character in the film made a terrible mistake.
40. Robbie is responsible for taking care of his goldfish.
41. In science we are learning about reversible changes.
42. Luckily the muddy coat was washable.
43. The colouring of the butterfly's wings was remarkable.
44. The fairy cakes were irresistible.
45. The teacher asked a reliable pupil to help her carry the books.

Test 5
1–18. act, action, actor
government, govern, governor
operate, cooperate, operator
disapprove, approval, prove
given, forgiveness, give
passenger, pass, passage

21–30. Possible answers include:
21. A fortnight of heavy rain brought the drought to an end.
22. The scientists made a breakthrough in their research.
23. The girls didn't have enough money to buy the big packet of sweets.
24. It was a very thoughtful gift.
25. The answer to the maths problem was nought.
26. Mum brought cakes to the picnic.
27. We live roughly halfway between here and the school.
28. Katie was captivated throughout the play.
29. The boys were thoroughly exhausted after the football match.
30. She popped another swimsuit in the suitcase as an afterthought.

19–50. Answers might include:
19. childlike
20. electrical
21. publication
22. covered
23. heroic
24. painful
25. daylight
26. unpack
27. joyful
28. pressure
29. hopeful
30. undertake
31. unusual
32. development
33. prisoner
34. discount
35. favourite
36. musical
37. assistant
38. agreement
39. medicine
40. calling
41. signature
42. interesting
43. infection
44. unclear
45. disturbing
46. relaxing
47. unchanged
48. export
49. handmade
50. lonely

Test 6
1–25. Answers might include:
1. trustworthy
2. massive
3. hidden
4. wrinkle
5. rush
6. mock
7. baffled
8. captivate
9. fling
10. unsettle
11. concur
12. persevere
13. grow
14. flourish
15. respond
16. disobedient
17. chilly
18. quarrelled
19. restrain
20. pondered
21 arranged
22. drenched
23. certain
24. declined
25. renowned

Test 7
1. walked
2. spoke
3. went
4. wished
5. slept
6. was
7. bought
8. wept
9. gave
10. lost
11. worried
12. found
13. whispered
14. lived
15. swept
16. saved
17. cried
18. leapt
19. thought
20. ran
21. woke
22. feel
23. saved
24. tries
25. caught
26. teaches
27. worked
28. grew
29. knew
30. came
31. Lauren always won running races.
32. Sam played football, even when it was raining.
33. Nakia's school uniform was navy blue.
34. Dad enjoyed visiting Spain because he could speak Spanish.
35. The boys tidied their rooms every Saturday morning.
36. My sister made a terrible mess when she was looking for something.
37. We visited the castle during our holiday.
38. Bhavin often left his schoolbag on the bus by mistake.
39. I usually got to school on time.
40. I read loads of books during the summer holidays.

1. bravely
2. hopefully
3. rapidly
4. colourfully
5. nervously
6. rudely
7. lately
8. surely
9. angrily
10. daintily
11. greedily
12. dreamily
13. soon
14. unsteadily
15. loudly
16. proudly
17. neatly
18. Suddenly
19. Almost
20. brightly
21–40. Sentences will vary.

Test 9

1. am
2. love
3. were
4. watch
5. fly
6. laughs
7. says
8. try
9. play
10. is
11. was
12. is
13. were
14. is
15. "Are/Were
16. was
17. are
18. is
19. are
20. were
21. was
22. Are
23. Were
24. eat
25. thinks
26. worry
27. sleeps
28. helps
29. were
30. win

Test 10

1. darken
2. formalise
3. realise
4. tighten
5. domesticate
6. apologise
7. purify
8. ripen
9. notify
10. publicise
11. replicate
12. specialise
13. standardise
14. medicate
15. activate
16. classify
17. captivate
18. glorify
19. simplify
20. awaken
21. clarify
22. pacify
23. implicate
24. intensify
25. beautify
26. memorise
27. dramatise
28. donate
29. televise
30. liquefy
31. tighten
32. advertise
33. fixate
34. finalise
35. sharpen
36. hospitalise
37. acidify
38. signify
39. moisten
40. carbonate/carbonise

Test 11

1–10. Correct sentences are: 2, 3, 6, 7, 8.

11. The football team (who had won their past four matches) hoped to win the cup.
12. My uncle is a funny man – he works in a circus after all – but can still be quite strict.
13. Our new classmate (who has just arrived from Spain) sits next to Charlie.
14. Rory said – and I heard him quite clearly – that he would be home in time for dinner.
15. The house (built when Queen Victoria was still on the throne) had seen better days.
16. I'm not happy about the playroom – my playroom – being turned into a nursery for my baby brother.
17. My sister – who is hardly ever ill – is in bed with a bad cold.
18. The author's latest book – *When We Were Witches* – is a best-seller.
19. It rained all day and (as a result) the cricket match was cancelled.
20. I wore my thick coat (the one with the fur collar) to stay warm in the snow.
21. We iced the cake – the size of a pillow – with bright pink frosting.
22. Molly (last year's fastest sprinter) is hoping to win the race.
23. Daniel (Joe's twin) is coming over for tea.
24. Eve (and her little dog) are always welcome.
25. The man's car – which was brand new – pulled into the car park.

Test 12

```
r e l u c t a n t l y                
                i                    
      s s o l i d l y           p    
      u       i                 a    
h u r r i e d l y               i    
c     e   u       y         c n      
m a d l y     d           h f        
l y       e p             e u        
m e s s i l y           q a l        
s o f t l y       a y     f u p l    
o     y       y h o r r i b l y      
t     y       f           e c y      
h e a v i l y u         s k          
l     i   l             h l          
l     p o l i t e l y                
y     p   y             y            
          a                          
          h                          
```

Test 13

1. Perhaps
2. Maybe
3. definitely
4. certainly
5. obviously
6. Surely
7. doubtless
8. possibly
9. clearly
10. probably
11–20. Possible answers include:
11. get wet.
12. be late for school.
13. always do your homework.
14. buy a magazine.
15. be very cold.
16. hide her sweets.
17. go to live with new familes.
18. go to the beach.
19. learn to drive.
20. get lost.

Test 14

1–20. Direct speech: 1, 2, 4, 7, 8, 11, 12, 14, 16, 19, 20
Reported speech: 3, 5, 6, 9, 10, 13, 15, 17, 18

21–30. Sentences may vary.
21. The twins asked for a drink.
22. Mr Parsons said he loved Robbie's picture.
23. Maddie shouted at me to get out of her room.
24. Dad contentedly said he couldn't eat another thing.
25. Abdul asked Matthew if he had seen the rainbow.
26. Mum said she needed to buy eggs and milk.
27. Gran reminded me to take my packed lunch.
28. The man asked what time the train would leave.
29. Mr Cooper explained that Henry VIII had six wives.
30. The woman asked for a book of stamps.

Test 15

1. brass, bronze, gold, platinum, silver
2. apple, banana, blueberry, clementine, grape
3. ten, thirteen, thirty, twenty, two
4. jaguar, leopard, lion, lynx, panther
5. beige, black, blue, brown, burgundy
6. sparrow, starling, swallow, swan, swift
7. cabbage, carrot, cauliflower, corn, courgette
8. April, August, January, July, June
9. shirt, shoe, skirt, sock, sweater
10. anchovy, angelfish, archerfish, barfish, barracuda
11–25. Possible answers include:
11. main major make
12. port post power
13. baby bake band
14. fabric farm feather
15. trail train trampoline
16. caper cast catch
17. rail rally rare
18. ugly unappetising under
19. acorn addition again
20. beam bear beat
21. daisy danger dare
22. limb line lint
23. bulb bundle burn
24. climb cling clip
25. dank dart dawn
26–35. Possible definitions include:
26. angry
27. expressed few words
28. having several possible meanings
29. understanding the thoughts and feelings of other people
30. someone with no permanent home
31. an odour or scent
32. a cliff with a vertical face
33. angry dispute or argument
34. unaware of something
35. to copy something

Test 16

1–10. Possible answers include:
1. Rachael did not like the soup.

We know this because she pulled a face, which is what people do when they don't like the taste of something. She also pushed the bowl away because she did not want it near her.

2. I think that Will did not do very well in the test and when he saw his score he realised that he should have spent the weekend studying for the test, instead of playing football.

3. I think Callum's school report was not very good. I think this because his mum flung it on the table and looked fiercely at him, which suggests she was angry with him about it.

4. I think there was a cat or kitten in the box because something made the lid move and cats and kittens make a mewing sound.

5. I think Dad is impatient because the traffic jam is making him late for something important. I think this because he keeps looking at his watch to see what time it is and is drumming his fingers, which people often do when they are frustrated. People also sigh heavily when things are not going as they want and they are getting cross.

6. I think that the action takes place at night because the boys have to feel their way, which suggests that they can't see where they are going. They also hear an owl and owls fly at night.

7. I think Emma put her sweets away because she did not want to share them with her friends. I think this because she put them away quickly as soon as she saw her friends coming, as if she did not want them to see that she had sweets.

8. I think Tommy is delighted to see his father because when someone's face 'lights up' it means they are happy. I think he ran towards him in excitement, perhaps to have a hug.

9. I think the woman may have had an accident because it says she is reluctant to look at the bumper which means she is worried it has been damaged. Also she is trembling, and people often tremble when they have had a shock, such as an accident.

10. I think Clara was sent to bed because she had been sneezing a lot and people who sneeze a lot might be ill and need to go to bed.

Test 17

1. here
2. hear
3. their
4. there

5. too
6. to
7. great
8. grate
9. brake
10. break
11. allowed
12. aloud
13. led
14. lead
15. Where
16. wear
17. eight
18. ate
19. sight
20. site

21–40. Sentences will vary.

Test 18

1. mission
2. magician
3. confusion
4. competition
5. station
6. pollution
7. session
8. extension
9. optician
10. explosion
11. possession
12. completion
13. diction
14. profession
15. emotion
16. reduction
17. contribution
18. mansion
19. education
20. proportion
21. politician
22. exclusion
23. fiction
24. discussion
25. devotion
26. attention
27. lotion
28. distribution
29. position
30. foundation
31. electrician
32. direction
33. oppression
34. transfusion
35. nation
36. translation
37. repetition
38. fraction
39. constitution
40. promotion
41. petition
42. deletion
43. occupation
44. infusion
45. demonstration
46. intuition
47. corrosion
48. motion
49. opposition
50. passion

Test 19

1. The children who live next door came round to play.

2. I was reading a book when the phone rang.

3. The ball that broke the window belongs to my brother.

4. All of the roads which lead into town were full of cars.

5. We live next door to a family whose pet rabbits keep escaping.

6. That is the house that we used to live in.

7. Who was that boy whom you were talking to?

8. That is the stadium where my favourite team plays.

9. I left some questions which were too difficult for me.

10. Chloe was surprised when her cousins knocked on the door.

11. The picture that won the art prize was amazing.

12. My older sister is a person whose bedroom is always tidy.

13. There was a huge puddle where we needed to cross the road.

14. The actor who starred in the new film is my favourite.

15. We were so cold when it began to snow.

16–30. Possible answers include:

16. Those are the friends whom we met at the park.

17. I was excited when the party invitation arrived.

18. He showed me a shop where you can buy the best sweets.

19. Mark is a student who always gets full marks in tests.

20. Mum spoke to the man whose car was blocking our driveway.

21. We caught a train which arrived at the station on time.

22. The children filed into the hall, which was full of teachers and parents.

23. The little girl, who was upset, cuddled her teddy.

24. The branches of the tree, which were laden with apples, sagged almost to the ground.

25. The children in 5F, whose classroom had been flooded, had their lessons in the school library.

26. I was amazed when I opened the parcel.

27. This is the road that leads to my house.

28. The author who wrote this book is my favourite.

29. I glared at the man whose dog was barking.

30. It was Sarah who wrote me that email.

Test 20

1. firstly
2. Secondly
3. Lastly
4. from
5. away
6. nearby
7. usually
8. sometimes
9. later
10. yesterday

11–25. Possible answers include:

11. my little sister behaved very well.
12. like to play outside.
13. watched films
14. We found a great fish and chip shop
15. my best friend.
16. Japan
17. go home.
18. the train carriage.
19. I've always loved animals.
20. we were learning about rivers.
21. cold in June.
22. marks our work carefully.
23. be time for bed.
24. we are going to Spain on holiday.
25. she has moved house twice.

Test 21

1–35. Answers will vary.

127

Test 22

1. Tree <u>boughs bobbed</u> in the wind.
2. The <u>crafty cat crawled</u> towards the bird.
3. There was a spell of <u>wet, windy weather</u>.
4. The old gate was <u>rust red</u>.
5. My <u>sister's sweet smile</u> cheered me up.
6. <u>Bobbie's balloon burst</u> with a pop.
7. Maggie sank into the <u>plump, purple pillow</u>.
8. The <u>creepy castle</u> loomed over us.
9. Chris won a <u>Super Student</u> award.
10. <u>Paula picked pink paint</u>.
11. metaphor
12. simile
13. metaphor
14. simile
15. simile
16. simile
17. simile
18. metaphor
19. simile
20. metaphor

21–30. Possible answers include:
21. The branches reached for me.
22. The mountain glared down at us.
23. The flowers danced in the breeze.
24. The waves tickled my feet.
25. The windows stared blankly.
26. The birds chattered noisily in the trees.
27. The moon smiled down at us.
28. The time marched on.
29. The wind whispered.
30. The sun embraced us with its warmth.

Test 23

1. crackle
2. whistle
3. sniff
4. rattle
5. smack
6. clatter
7. drip
8. whoosh
9. rip
10. scrape
11. hiss
12. creak
13. howl
14. wail
15. rustle

Test 24

1. Our it
2. her
3. us
4. he
5. they
6. I we
7. it
8. them
9. my
10. him
11. they
12. it
13. him
14. him
15. I
16. they
17. she
18. we
19. her
20. them
21. she
22. it
23. they
24. us/them
25. she
26. he
27. we
28. it
29. him
30. they

Test 25

1. redirect
2. decode
3. refund
4. overlook
5. disappear
6. overheat
7. misinterpret
8. misinform/overinform
9. deport
10. disagree
11. disable
12. reprint
13. disbelieve
14. reunite
15. recall

16–30. Possible answers include:
16. Sam disobeyed the school rule and ran in the corridor.
17. It is easy to misunderstand tricky new topics in class.
18. Mum had to overtake the cyclist.
19. Most people disapprove of dropping litter.
20. If you overload that shelf it might break.
21. We had to defrost our freezer.
22. If we misbehave, our teacher will be disappointed with us.
23. I did not let the difficult questions discourage me.
24. The shopkeeper was careful not to overcharge her customers.
25. We were disappointed when our snowman melted.
26. You must disconnect the water supply before fixing the leak.
27. I have misplaced by school bag.
28. I did not know how to react to the news.
29. We managed to overcome the problem.
30. We are going to rebuild the shed that blew down in the storm.

Test 26

1. mine
2. his
3. ours
4. yours
5. ours
6. theirs
7. his
8. yours
9. theirs
10. mine
11. hers
12. his
13. ours
14. hers
15. hers
16. that
17. who
18. which
19. whom
20. who
21. that
22. whom
23. who
24. that
25. whose
26. that
27. which
28. that
29. who
30. that

Test 27

1–10. Correct sentences: 1, 4, 5, 6, 8.
11. "Don't wake Dad," whispered Mum.
12. "When will it stop raining?" wondered Jack.
13. "This isn't the one I wanted!" complained the man.
14. "You're wrong!" argued Sophie.
15. The teacher explained, "You need to measure carefully."
16. "Is this platform 4?" queried the woman.
17. Dad insisted, "You must eat your vegetables."
18. "Have you seen her dress?" gossiped the girls.
19. Will giggled, "That's so funny!"
20. "I'm thirsty," grumbled Elsa.

21–30. Possible answers include:
21. moaned
22. whispered
23. screeched
24. asked
25. gasped

---

26. enquired
27. argued
28. explained
29. worried
30. complained
31–40. Answers will vary.

Test 28

1–10. Correct sentences: 1, 5, 7, 8, 9, 10
11. train's
12. children's
13. students'
14. Auntie Pat's
15. pigeons'
16. fairies'
17. queen's
18. girls'
19. boy's
20. dog's
21. couldn't
22. I'm
23. she's
24. they're
25. we've
26. shan't
27. won't
28. should've
29. it's
30. you'll

Test 29

1–10. Answers will vary.

Adjective	+er	+est
11–12. small	smaller	smallest
13–14. kind	kinder	kindest
15–16. brave	braver	bravest
17–18. big	bigger	biggest
19–20. bright	brighter	brightest
21–22. lovely	lovelier	loveliest
23–24. funny	funnier	funniest
25–26. rude	ruder	rudest
27–28. fit	fitter	fittest
29–30. young	younger	youngest

31–40. Answers will vary.
41–50. Answers will vary.

Test 30

1. because
2. and
3. Although
4. so
5. while
6. Because
7. So
8. After
9. until
10. but
11. because
12. while
13. and
14. so
15. although
16. but
17. because
18. Because
19. Despite
20. Before

21–30. Answers may vary:
21. It was windy and a tree blew down.
22. We missed the bus, so we had to wait for the next one.
23. I looked for my phone and it was under my bed.
24. We clapped and cheered when our team scored a goal.
25. We looked at the stars when night fell.
26. I wanted strawberry ice-cream, but the shop only had vanilla.
27. Joe entered the competition and he won!
28. It was not raining although the sky was full of black clouds.
29. The woman sat down for a rest because her shopping bags were heavy.
30. I told her the secret because I trusted her.